Acknowledgements

The publishers would like to thank the following
for permission to reproduce photographs

AA Photo Library: 37 top right; Aerofilms Limited: 13, 30 all;
Bryan & Cherry Alexander Photography: 58 middle, 61 middle;
Austin Brown/Aviation Picture Library: 66 right;
British Petroleum Shipping Ltd (Fotoflite): 67 right;
Chorley & Handford: 7 all, 32 all, 34;
Comstock Photo Library: 54, 58 bottom left, 59 middle,
60 bottom middle, 61 right;
English Heritage Photographic Library: 37 bottom left;
The Environmental Picture Library: 36, 63 left; FLPA:
60 bottom right;
Greg Evans International; 37 top left, 58 bottom middle,
58 bottom right, 59 bottom left;
Robert Harding Picture Library Ltd: 33 top, 33 middle,
60 top right, 62 top;
Holt Studios International: 31 all;
The Hutchison Library: 33 bottom, 62 bottom;
David Keith Jones/Images of Africa Photobank: 59 bottom right;
Mark Mason: 4 top right, 5;
National Remote Sensing Centre (Airphotogroup): 4 top left;
Marilyn O'Brien: 37 bottom right;
Christine Osborne Pictures: 60 bottom left;
Port of Felixstowe: 67 left;   Rex Features: 62 middle;
Science Photo Library: 14, 56 middle, 57, 60 top left, 66 left;
Skyscan: 34 right; Still Pictures: 56 bottom;
The Telegraph Colour Library: 59 bottom middle,
60 top middle, 65;
Tropix Photographic Library: 63 right;
United States Atlantic Fleet Submarine Force:,
Public Affairs Office 55.

Cover image:
Tom Van Sant / Geosphere Project, Santa Monica ,
Science Photo Library.

The illustrations are by Chapman Bounford, Hard Lines,
Mike Harkins, and Gary Hinks.

The page design is by Adrian Smith.

OXFORD
UNIVERSITY PRESS

Great Clarendon Street, Oxford OX2 6DP

Oxford University Press is a department of the University of Oxford.
It furthers the University's objective of excellence in research, scholarship,
and education by publishing worldwide in

Oxford New York

Auckland Bangkok Buenos Aires Cape Town Chennai
Dar es Salaam Delhi Hong Kong Istanbul Karachi Kolkata
Kuala Lumpur Madrid Melbourne Mexico City Mumbai Nairobi
São Paulo Shanghai Taipei Tokyo Toronto

Oxford is a registered trade mark of Oxford University Press
in the UK and in certain other countries

© Oxford University Press 1996

First published 1996
Reprinted 1996, with corrections 1997,
1998 (twice), with corrections 1999, 2000, 2001 (twice), 2002 (twice)

© Maps copyright Oxford University Press

ISBN 0 19 831793 X (paperback)   ISBN 0 19 831834 0 (hardback)

Printed in Italy by G. Canale & C. S.p.A. - Borgaro T.se - Turin

THE OXFORD Junior ATLAS

Editorial Adviser

Patrick Wiegand

Oxford University Press

2 Contents

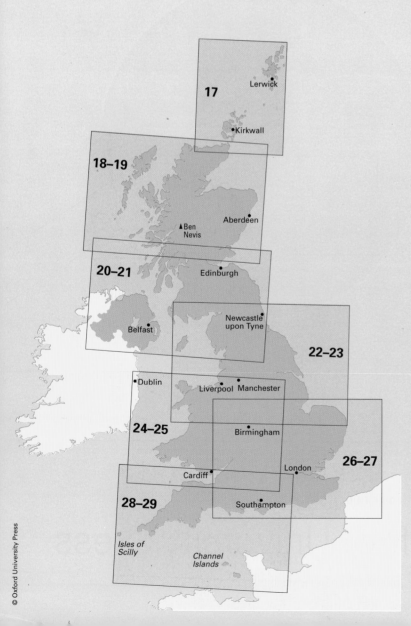

Contents

Continents and Poles

The World

Liskeard **28** C3
Lismore *island* **18** D1
Lithuania 38 D2
Littlehampton **29** G3
Little Minch *sound* **18** C2
Little Ouse *river* **27** E3

Index

4 Round Earth

A globe shows the Earth as a sphere.

A globe is a model of the Earth.
Globes are accurate but difficult to use.
You can only see one part of the world at a time.

Globes have two sets of lines to help us describe where places are on the Earth.
All the lines are numbered and some have special names.

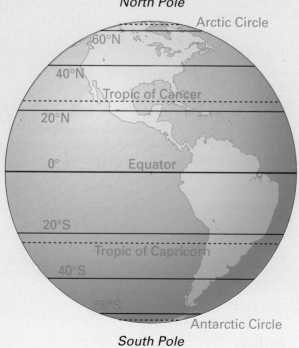

North Pole
Arctic Circle
60°N
40°N
Tropic of Cancer
20°N
0° Equator
20°S
Tropic of Capricorn
40°S
60°S
Antarctic Circle
South Pole

These are lines of latitude.

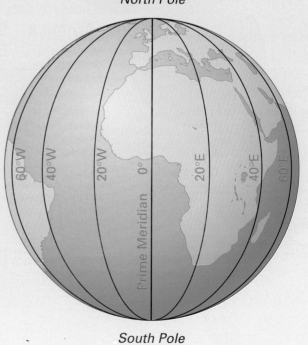

North Pole
60°W 40°W 20°W 0° 20°E 40°E 60°E
Prime Meridian
South Pole

These are lines of longitude.

A world map shows the Earth on a flat piece of paper.

It is difficult to show shapes from a round Earth on a flat map.

Most world maps do not show Antarctica clearly.

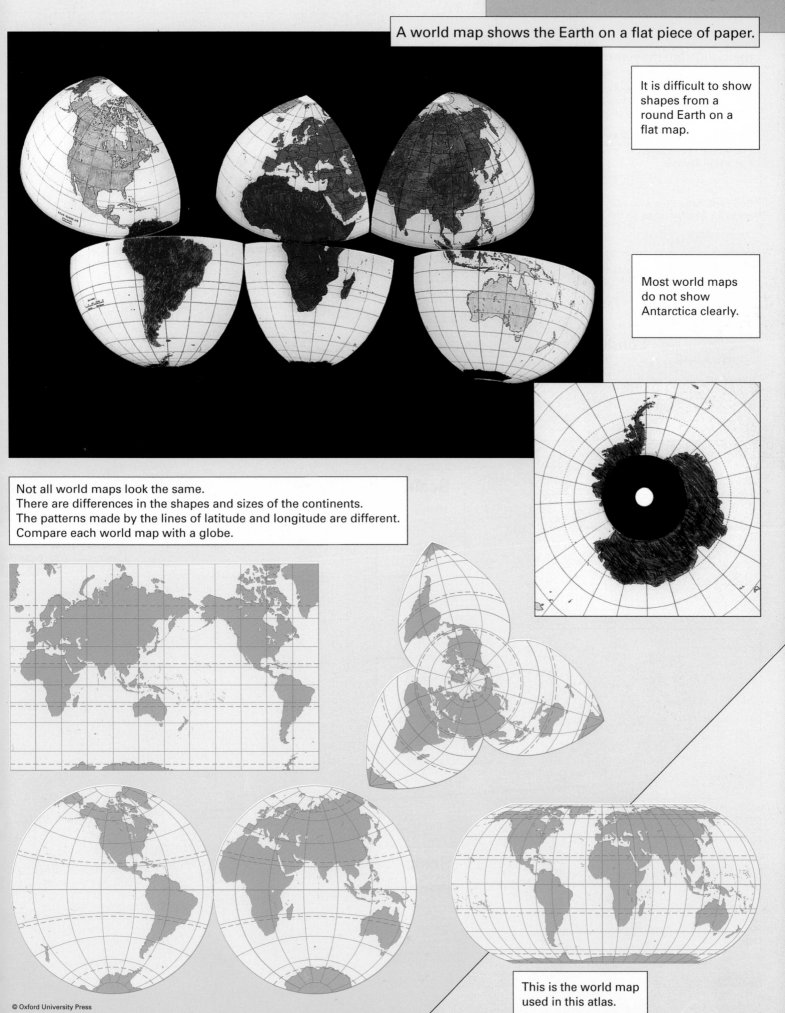

Not all world maps look the same.
There are differences in the shapes and sizes of the continents.
The patterns made by the lines of latitude and longitude are different.
Compare each world map with a globe.

This is the world map used in this atlas.

6 Scale

Atlas maps have to be much, much smaller than the countries they show.

One centimetre on a map has to stand for many kilometres on the ground.

Every map in this atlas has a sign like this :

12 km
one cm

One centimetre on a map with *this* sign would stand for 12 kilometres on the ground.

You can see more detail on some maps than others. The amount of detail depends on the **scale** of the map.
See how the British Isles become smaller as the scale changes on the maps below.

Scale

20 km
one cm

Scale

100 km
one cm

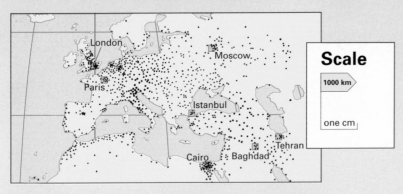

Scale

1000 km
one cm

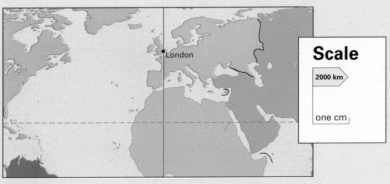

Scale

2000 km
one cm

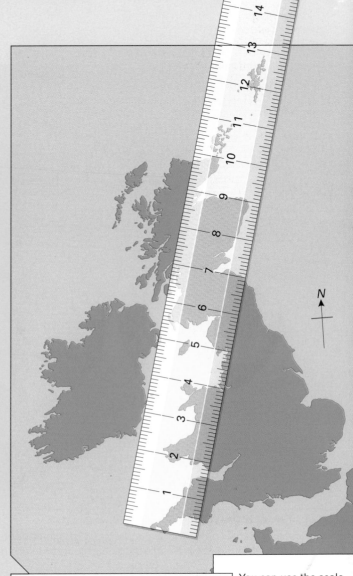

N

100 km
one cm

One centimetre on the map measures 100 kilometres on the ground.

0   100   200   300   400 km

1   2   3   4   5

You can use the scale information to measure distances on maps. Great Britain is approximately 1000 km from north to south. Check it with your ruler.

Small maps like this on some pages of the atlas help you to compare the size of other countries with the British Isles.

Most people in Britain live in towns.
Some towns are large, others are small.
In many parts of the country several towns have grown so large that they have joined to form one huge built-up area.

Each size of settlement has its own map symbol and style of lettering for the place name. Only the largest settlements are marked on atlas maps.

People live in settlements of different sizes.

Largest towns
100 000 - 1 million people

Leeds

Largest built-up areas
more than 1 million people

Walsall
Sutton
Coldfield
West
Bromwich
Warley
Birmingham
Solihull
Kenilworth

Large towns
25 000 - 100 000 people

Bath   R. Avon

Small towns
10 000 - 25 000 people

Marden

Small towns and villages
fewer than 10 000 people

Many very small towns and villages are not shown on atlas maps.

On atlas maps the height of the land above sea level is shown by colours.

Peak or highest point
with exact height given in metres

Highest mountain
only a few parts of Great Britain
are over 1000 metres high

Mountains
high and steep rocky slopes

Moors and uplands
high land with open views

Lake
water with land all around

Hills
smooth sloping landscapes with
winding rivers

Low land
wide plains, often near the sea

Coast
where the land and sea meet

Island
land with water
all around

Sea
tidal salt water

Key

Land height measured in
metres above sea level

	more than 1000m
	500 - 1000m
	200 - 500m
	100 - 200m
	less than 100m
	sea

HIGH
MOUNTAINS peak

MOUNTAINS

MOUNTAINS

lake

HILLS

MOORS
AND
UPLANDS

LOW
LAND

coast

river

HILLS

island

LOW
LAND

sea

coast

The colours used to show land height
on this page are the same as
those used for the maps of the
British Isles on pages 17–29.
Different colours are used for
other parts of the world.

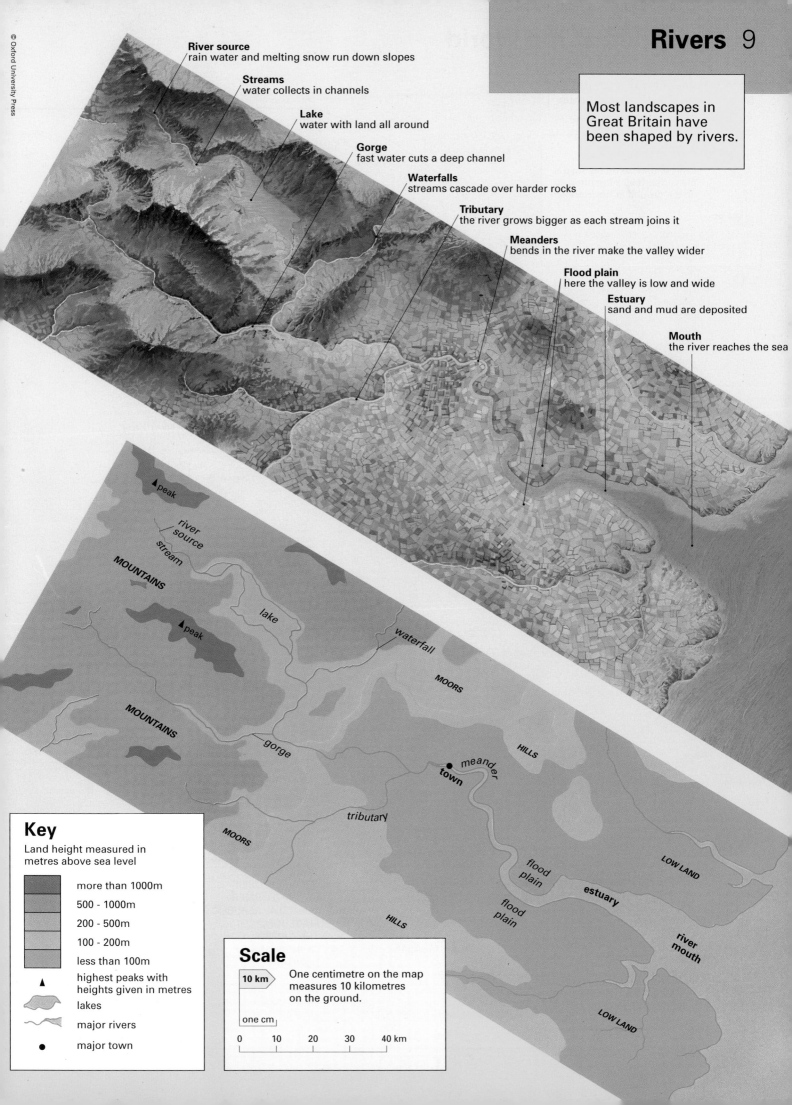

River source
rain water and melting snow run down slopes

Streams
water collects in channels

Lake
water with land all around

Gorge
fast water cuts a deep channel

Waterfalls
streams cascade over harder rocks

Tributary
the river grows bigger as each stream joins it

Meanders
bends in the river make the valley wider

Flood plain
here the valley is low and wide

Estuary
sand and mud are deposited

Mouth
the river reaches the sea

Most landscapes in
Great Britain have
been shaped by rivers.

peak

river
source

stream

MOUNTAINS

peak

lake

waterfall

MOORS

MOUNTAINS

HILLS

gorge

town

meander

tributary

MOORS

flood
plain

flood
plain

estuary

LOW LAND

HILLS

river
mouth

LOW LAND

Key

Land height measured in
metres above sea level

more than 1000m

500 - 1000m

200 - 500m

100 - 200m

less than 100m

▲ highest peaks with
heights given in metres

lakes

major rivers

• major town

Scale

10 km

One centimetre on the map
measures 10 kilometres
on the ground.

one cm

0   10   20   30   40 km

A country is a land with its own people and its own laws.

Scale

1050 km

One centimetre on the map measures 1050 kilometres on the ground at the Equator.

one cm

| 0 | 1050 | 2100 | 3150 | 4200 km |

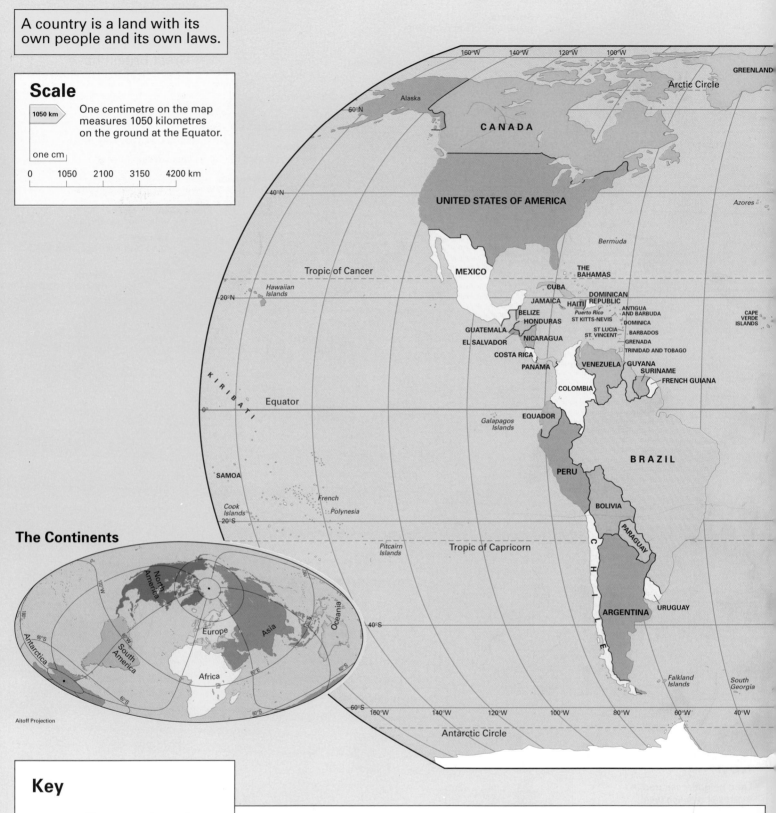

The Continents

Aitoff Projection

Key

CANADA — The names of countries are shown with this type of lettering.

Countries that are too small to be named on the map are shown by the first few letters of their name.

 These colours are used to show where one country ends and another begins.

A	ALBANIA	CZ	CZECH REPUBLIC	N	NETHERLANDS
AR	ARMENIA	F	FYROM (FORMER	Q	QATAR
AU	AUSTRIA		YUGOSLAV REPUBLIC OF	R	ROMANIA
AZ	AZERBAIJAN		MACEDONIA)	S	SLOVAKIA
B	BELGIUM	G	THE GAMBIA	SL	SLOVENIA
BD	BRUNEI DARUSSALAM	G-B	GUINEA-BISSAU	SW	SWITZERLAND
BE	BENIN	H	HUNGARY	T	TAJIKISTAN
BH	BOSNIA-HERZEGOVINA	IS	ISRAEL	TU	TURKMENISTAN
BU	BURKINA	L	LEBANON	U	UGANDA
C	CROATIA	LI	LITHUANIA	UAE	UNITED ARAB EMIRATES
CAR	CENTRAL AFRICAN REPUBLIC	LU	LUXEMBOURG	Y	YUGOSLAVIA
				ZIM	ZIMBABWE

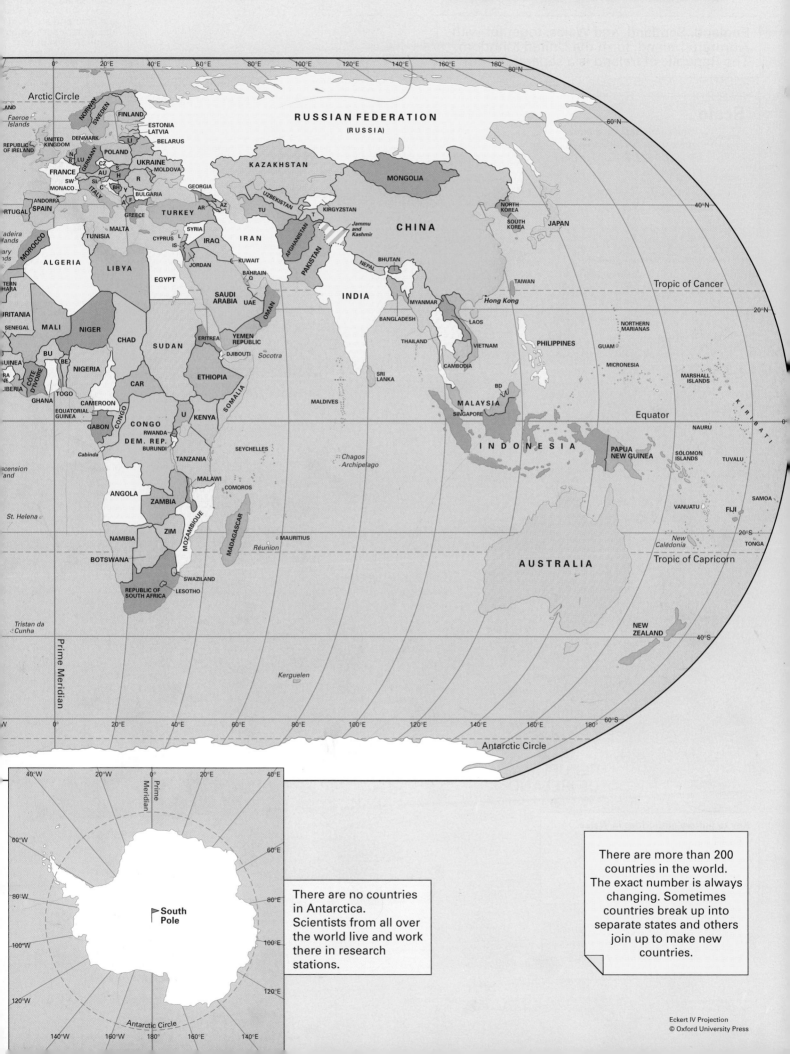

Arctic Circle

Faeroe
Islands

AND

RUSSIAN FEDERATION
(RUSSIA)

NORWAY
SWEDEN
FINLAND

REPUBLIC
OF IRELAND

UNITED
KINGDOM
DENMARK
ESTONIA
LATVIA
BELARUS

LI
POLAND

N
LU
GERMANY
FRANCE
AU
SW
MONACO
SL
C
ITALY
BH
Y
A
F
L
GREECE
MALTA
TUNISIA
CYPRUS
IS
SYRIA
LEBANON

UKRAINE
MOLDOVA

GEORGIA
BULGARIA

TURKEY
AR
AZ

KAZAKHSTAN

MONGOLIA

NORTH
KOREA
SOUTH
KOREA
JAPAN

80°N

60°N

40°N

UZBEKISTAN

TU

IRAN

IRAQ
KUWAIT
JORDAN
BAHRAIN
Q

SAUDI
ARABIA
UAE
OMAN

T
KIRGYZSTAN
AFGHANISTAN
PAKISTAN

NEPAL
BHUTAN

Jammu
and
Kashmir

CHINA

TAIWAN
Hong Kong

Tropic of Cancer

20°N

INDIA
MYANMAR
BANGLADESH
LAOS

THAILAND
VIETNAM
CAMBODIA

NORTHERN
MARIANAS
GUAM

MICRONESIA

MARSHALL
ISLANDS

ANDORRA
SPAIN
PORTUGAL
MOROCCO
adeira
ands
ary
nds
TERN
HARA
URITANIA
SENEGAL
BU
GUINEA
RA
BE
LIBERIA
CÔTE
D'IVOIRE
TOGO
GHANA

ALGERIA
LIBYA
EGYPT

MALI
NIGER
CHAD
SUDAN
NIGERIA
CAR
CAMEROON
EQUATORIAL
GUINEA

ERITREA
YEMEN
REPUBLIC
DJIBOUTI
Socotra

ETHIOPIA
SOMALIA

MALDIVES

SRI
LANKA

Chagos
Archipelago

MALAYSIA
SINGAPORE
BD

I N D O N E S I A

PHILIPPINES

PAPUA
NEW GUINEA

SOLOMON
ISLANDS

NAURU

KIRIBATI

TUVALU

Equator
0°

GABON
CONGO
CONGO
DEM. REP.
RWANDA
BURUNDI
U
KENYA
TANZANIA
SEYCHELLES

Cabinda

scension
and

St. Helena

ANGOLA
ZAMBIA
MALAWI
COMOROS
ZIM
MOZAMBIQUE
MADAGASCAR
Réunion
MAURITIUS

NAMIBIA
BOTSWANA
SWAZILAND
REPUBLIC OF
SOUTH AFRICA
LESOTHO

AUSTRALIA

VANUATU
New
Calédonia

FIJI
SAMOA
TONGA

20°S
Tropic of Capricorn

Tristan da
Cunha

Kerguelen

NEW
ZEALAND

40°S

Prime Meridian

60°S

Antarctic Circle

There are no countries
in Antarctica.
Scientists from all over
the world live and work
there in research
stations.

South
Pole

There are more than 200
countries in the world.
The exact number is always
changing. Sometimes
countries break up into
separate states and others
join up to make new
countries.

England, Scotland, and Wales, together with Northern Ireland, form the United Kingdom. The Republic of Ireland is a separate country.

England is divided into counties and some new unitary authorities. Wales and Scotland are divided into unitary authorities. Northern Ireland is divided into districts.

The Republic of Ireland divided into counties.

Scale

45 km ▷ One centimetre on the map measures 45 kilometres on the ground

one cm

| 0 | 45 | 90 | 135 | 180 km |

Key to unitary authorities in Scotland

1 West Dunbartonshire
2 East Dunbartonshire
3 North Lanarkshire
4 Glasgow City
5 East Renfrewshire
6 Renfrewshire
7 Inverclyde
8 Clackmannanshire
9 Falkirk
10 West Lothian
11 City of Edinburgh
12 Midlothian
13 East Lothian
14 North Ayrshire
15 East Ayrshire
16 Dundee City

Key to districts in Northern Ireland

1	Belfast	14	Fermanagh
2	Newtownabbey	15	Omagh
3	Carrickfergus	16	Cookstown
4	Castlereagh	17	Magherafelt
5	North Down	18	Strabane
6	Ards	19	Londonderry
7	Down	20	Limavady
8	Newry & Mourne	21	Coleraine
9	Banbridge	22	Ballymoney
10	Lisburn	23	Moyle
11	Craigavon	24	Ballymena
12	Armagh	25	Larne
13	Dungannon	26	Antrim

Republic of Ireland

United Kingdom

The British Isles consist of the two large islands of Great Britain and Ireland and a number of smaller islands.

Key to unitary authorities in Wales

1	Cardiff	8	Caerphilly
2	The Vale of Glamorgan	9	Blaenau Gwent
3	Bridgend	10	Monmouthshire
4	Swansea	11	Conwy
5	Neath Port Talbot	12	Denbighshire
6	Rhondda Cynon Taff	13	Flintshire
7	Merthyr Tydfil	14	Wrexham

Key to unitary authorities in England

1	Hartlepool	10	Bristol
2	Stockton-on-Tees	11	North Somerset
3	Middlesbrough	12	Bath and North East Somerset
4	Redcar and Cleveland	13	Luton
5	East Riding of Yorkshire	14	Milton Keynes
6	City of Kingston upon Hull	15	Leicester City
7	North Lincolnshire	16	Swindon
8	North East Lincolnshire	17	Windsor & Maidenhead
9	South Gloucestershire		

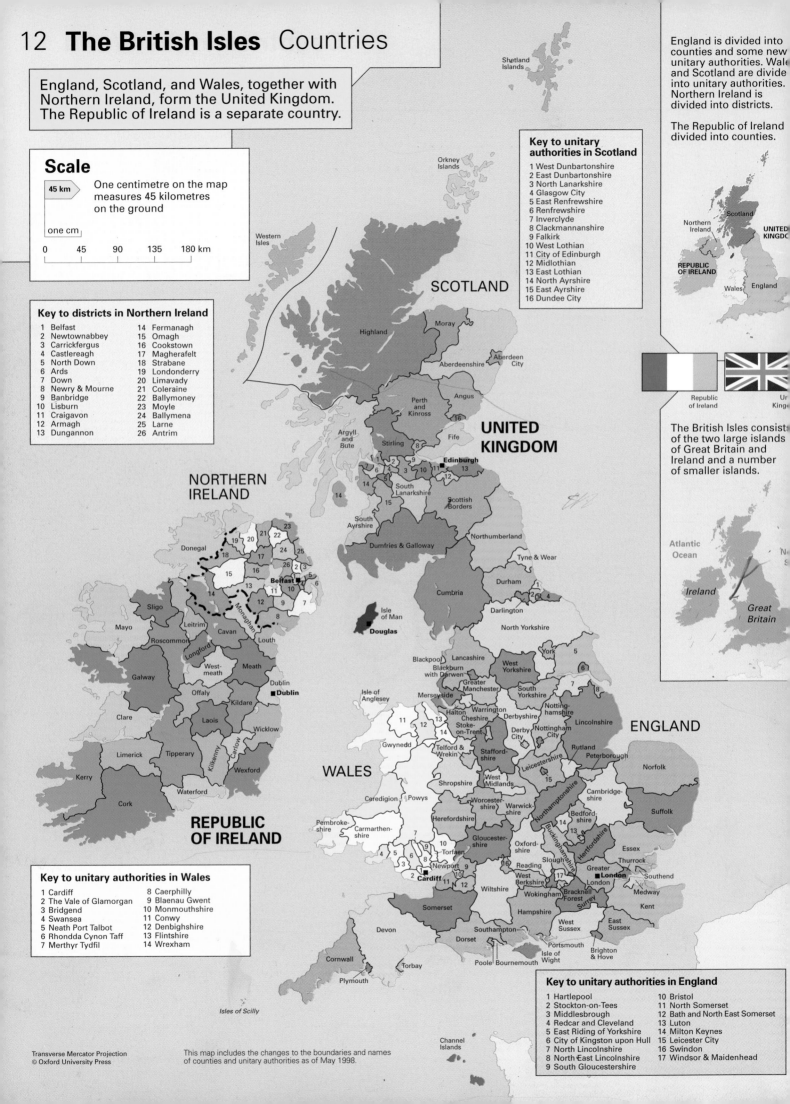

Transverse Mercator Projection
© Oxford University Press

This map includes the changes to the boundaries and names of counties and unitary authorities as of May 1998.

The highest parts of Great Britain are mostly in the north and west.

Key

Land height measured in metres above sea level

- more than 1000m
- 500 - 1000m
- 200 - 500m
- 100 - 200m
- less than 100m

▲ highest peaks with heights given in metres

lakes

major rivers

Scale

45 km

One centimetre on the map measures 45 kilometres on the ground.

one cm

| 0 | 45 | 90 | 135 | 180 km |

1344m ▲
Ben Nevis

The highest mountain in Great Britain is Ben Nevis (1344 metres or 4406 feet high) and the longest river is the Severn (354 kilometres or 220 miles long).

Transverse Mercator Projection
© Oxford University Press

Map labels

Shetland Islands

Orkney Islands

Cape Wrath

Outer Hebrides

Lewis

60°N

58°N

NORTHWEST HIGHLANDS

Great Glen

Loch Ness

River Spey

CAIRNGORMS

River Dee

Skye

1344m ▲ Ben Nevis

GRAMPIAN MOUNTAINS

River Tay

Mull

ATLANTIC OCEAN

Islay

Loch Lomond

River Clyde

Firth of Forth

56°N

SOUTHERN UPLANDS

Firth of Clyde

North Channel

River Tweed

CHEVIOT HILLS

ANTRIM MOUNTAINS

River Bann

Lough Neagh

River Erne

River Tyne

River Tees

LAKE DISTRICT

978m ▲ Scafell Pike

River Eden

PENNINES

NORTH YORK MOORS

River Ouse

Isle of Man

Irish Sea

54°N

852m ▲ Slieve Donard

River Boyne

Lough Corrib

River Shannon

River Liffey

River Aire

River Humber

The Wash

River Mersey

Anglesey

1085m ▲ Snowdon

WICKLOW MOUNTAINS

CAMBRIAN MOUNTAINS

River Dee

River Trent

THE FENS

River Wensum

River Barrow

River Suir

River Blackwater

1041m ▲ Carrauntoohill

Cardigan Bay

River Severn

River Avon

COTSWOLD HILLS

River Great Ouse

CHILTERN HILLS

River Stour

52°N

River Teifi

River Wye

River Usk

River Tywi

BRECON BEACONS

SALISBURY PLAIN

River Thames

NORTH DOWNS

St George's Channel

Bristol Channel

EXMOOR

River Exe

DARTMOOR

SOUTH DOWNS

Isle of Wight

Land's End

Isles of Scilly

English Channel

Strait of Dover

ATLANTIC OCEAN

Channel Islands

50°N

Prime Meridian

North Sea

0° 2°E 4°E

6°W 4°W 2°W 0°

10°W 8°W

Climate describes the average pattern of weather over a number of years.

Rainfall

The eastern parts of the British Isles are drier than the western parts. Mountains are wetter than lowlands.

Valentia

London

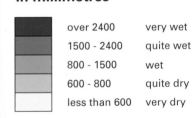

Average annual rainfall in millimetres

over 2400	very wet
1500 - 2400	quite wet
800 - 1500	wet
600 - 800	quite dry
less than 600	very dry

During the year many wet weather bands pass over the British Isles whilst southern Europe stays dry and warm. This is a satellite picture of the weather in western Europe on 6 August 1987.
Satellite pictures like this use colours that are different from the way the land looks to us.

Transverse Mercator Projection
© Oxford University Press

Average annual rainfall

The graphs show the amount of rainfall in Valentia and London for one year.
Valentia is wetter in winter. London has about the same amount of rainfall each month.

All the rain that falls in one year is the **annual rainfall**. Valentia has much more rain than London over the whole year.

Some years are wetter than others. The map shows the amount of rainfall you would expect in an average year.

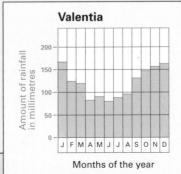

Valentia

Amount of rainfall in millimetres

200

150

100

50

0

J F M A M J J A S O N D

Months of the year

London

Amount of rainfall in millimetres

200

150

100

50

0

J F M A M J J A S O N D

Months of the year

January temperatures

In winter the mountains of Scotland are the coldest parts of the British Isles.

July temperatures

In summer the coasts of southern England are the warmest parts of the British Isles.

Scale

One centimetre on the map measures 100 kilometres on the ground.

100 km

one cm

0   100   200   300   400 km

In the British Isles it is usually colder in January than in July. However, some years might be very cold whilst others are quite warm. The maps show the temperatures you would expect in an average year.

Average temperatures in °Celsius

	above 16	hot
	14 - 16	very warm
	12 - 14	warm
	10 - 12	quite warm
	8 - 10	quite cool
	6 - 8	cool
	4 - 6	quite cold
	2 - 4	cold
	0 - 2	very cold
	below 0	freezing

Average temperatures in winter and summer

The graphs show the average temperatures each month for Stornoway, Braemar, London, and Penzance.
In all four places it is warmer in summer than in winter.

Summers in Stornoway and Braemar are much cooler than in London or Penzance.
Winter in Braemar is very cold.

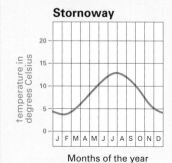

Stornoway

Months of the year

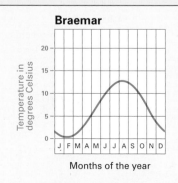

Braemar

Months of the year

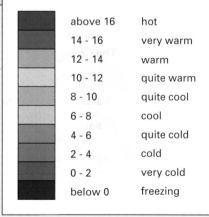

London

Months of the year

Penzance

Months of the year

Transverse Mercator Projection
© Oxford University Press

Maps that show all the most important features of the landscape are called **topographic** maps.

Key

- - - - -	international boundary
——	national boundary
━━━	motorways and main roads
──	railway
✈	main airport
∿	river
▨	lake
▲	peak or highest point

towns

▨	largest built-up areas
■	largest towns
●	large towns
•	other towns

Scale

45 km	One centimetre on the map measures 45 kilometres on the ground.

one cm

0	45	90	135	180 km

Land height

measured above sea level

	more than 1000m
	500 - 1000m
	200 - 500m
	100 - 200m
	less than 100m

Shetland Islands

Orkney Islands

Cape Wrath

Outer Hebrides

Lewis

Skye

Mull

NORTHWEST HIGHLANDS

Inverness

Great Glen
Loch Ness
River Spey

CAIRNGORMS

River Dee

Aberdeen

1344m ▲
Ben Nevis

GRAMPIAN MOUNTAINS

R. Tay

SCOTLAND

Loch Lomond

Dundee

Firth of Forth

Islay

Glasgow

Edinburgh

River Clyde

R. Tweed

NORTHERN IRELAND

Coleraine

Londonderry

R. Bann

ANTRIM MOUNTAINS

Larne

Ayr

SOUTHERN UPLANDS

CHEVIOT HILLS

UNITED KINGDOM

Lough Neagh

Belfast

Stranraer

Carlisle

River Eden

Newcastle upon Tyne

River Tyne

Sunderland

NORTH Sea

Sligo

River Erne

852m ▲
Slieve Donard

Isle of Man

LAKE DISTRICT
978m ▲
Scafell Pike

River Tees

Middlesbrough

NORTH YORK MOORS

REPUBLIC OF IRELAND

Lough Corrib

Irish Sea

PENNINES

River Ouse

54°N

ATLANTIC OCEAN

Galway

River Shannon

R. Boyne

R. Liffey

Dublin

Bradford
Leeds

River Aire

Kingston-upon-Hull

River Humber

WICKLOW MOUNTAINS

Anglesey

Holyhead

Manchester

Liverpool

River Mersey

Sheffield

Tiree

Barrow River

River Suir

Rosslare

1085m ▲
Snowdon

R. Dee

ENGLAND

R. Trent

Nottingham

The Wash

R. Wensum

1041m ▲
Carrauntoohill

River Blackwater

Cork

Fishguard

CAMBRIAN MOUNTAINS

River Severn

Leicester

THE FENS

Norwich

Cardigan Bay

Wolverhampton

Birmingham

Northampton

R. Great Ouse

R. Stour

WALES

River Teifi

River Tywi

BRECON BEACONS

River Usk

R. Wye

River Avon

COTSWOLD HILLS

Oxford

R. Thames

CHILTERN HILLS

Luton

London

Southend-on-Sea

Swansea

Cardiff

Newport

Bristol

SALISBURY PLAIN

Reading

NORTH DOWNS

Margate

Dover

Bristol Channel

EXMOOR

R. Exe

Southampton

Bournemouth

SOUTH DOWNS

Portsmouth

Brighton

Boulogne-sur-Mer

DARTMOOR

Exeter

Weymouth

Isle of Wight

Land's End

Penzance

Plymouth

Isles of Scilly

ATLANTIC OCEAN

English Channel

FRANCE

Cherbourg

le Havre

Rouen

R. Seine

Channel Islands

Prime Meridian

St George's Channel

North Channel

Firth of Clyde

© Oxford University Press
Transverse Mercator Projection

Scale

10 km

One centimetre on the map measures 10 kilometres on the ground.

one cm

| 0 | 10 | 20 | 30 | 40 km |

Key

- – – – – county or region boundary
- ——— motorway and main roads
- ——— railway
- ⊕ main airport
- ——— river
- lake
- ▲ peak or highest point

towns

- • other towns

Land height

measured above sea level

- 200-500m
- 100-200m
- less than 100m

ATLANTIC

OCEAN

3°W   C   2°W   D   1°W   E

Herma Ness

Haroldswick

Unst

Point of
Fethaland

Yell Sound

Yell

Fetlar

▲449m

Esha Ness

St Magnus
Bay

Fora
Ness

*Out
Skerries*

3

*Muckle
Roe*

Whalsay

Symbister

*Papa
Stour*

Mainland

SHETLAND
ISLANDS

Walls

Bressay

417m

The
Deeps

Lerwick

Foula ▲

Scalloway

60°N   60°N

Sumburgh
Head

4°W

B

2

Fair Isle

2

Mull Head

Papa Westray

North Ronaldsay

Westray

Sanday

Westray Firth

Rousay

Eday

Brough Head

Stronsay

Stronsay Firth

Shapinsay

59°N   59°N

Stromness

Mainland

Kirkwall

ORKNEY
ISLANDS

Kirkwall

Scapa

Ward Hill
479m ▲

*Scapa
Flow*

Rora Head

Hoy

South Ronaldsay

1   North   Sea   1

Pentland Firth

Dunnet Head *Stroma*

Strathy
Point

John o' Groats

Duncansby Head

Thurso

A   4°W   B   Halkirk   3°W   C   2°W   D   1°W   E

Transverse Mercator Projection
© Oxford University Press

Scale

10 km ▷ One centimetre on the map measures 10 kilometres on the ground.

one cm ▷

| 0 | 10 | 20 | 30 | 40 km |

Key

- – – – – county or region boundary
- ▬▬▬ motorway and main roads
- ───── railway
- ⊕ main airport
- ───── river
- ├┼┼┤ canal
- ◗ lake
- ▲ peak or highest point

towns

- built-up areas
- ■ largest towns
- ● large towns
- • other towns

Land height

measured above sea level

- more than 1000m
- 500-1000m
- 200-500m
- 100-200m
- less than 100m

ATLANTIC OCEAN

St Kilda

58°N

57°N

8°W

7°W

6°W

Butt of Lewis
Port of Ness

Lewis

Broad Bay

EYE PENINSULA

Stornoway

WESTERN ISLES

Hebrides

Scarp

Clisham 799m ▲

Taransay

Tarbert

Scalpay

Shiant Islands

Harris

The Minch

Eddrachi Ba

Enard Bay

Outer

Sound of Harris

Pabbay

Berneray

Little Minch

Rubha Hunish

Kilmaluag

Gairloch

Poolewe

Loch Maree

North Uist

Lochmaddy

Loch Snizort

The Storr 719m ▲

Loch Torridon

Ullap

NORTH

Benbecula

Dunvegan

Portree

Inner Sound

Raasay

HIGH

Skye

Scalpay

Kyle of Lochalsh

South Uist

CUILLIN HILLS

Broadford

River Shiel

Soay

Elgol

Eriskay

Canna

Calligarry

Barra

Kinloch

Mallaig

Lo Ark

Castlebay

Rhum

Arisaig

Eigg

Lo

Mingulay

Muck

Sound of Arisaig

Loch Shiel

Inner

Hebrides

Coll

Loch Linnhe

Tobermory

Lochaline

Tiree

Ulva

Ben More 967m ▲

Craignure

Lismore

Lo Etiv

Mull

Lochdon

Iona

Fionnphort

ROSS OF MULL

Sound of Mull

Oban

Kerrera

Ben Cruac

Lorn

Loch Awe

ARGY

Firth of

Scarba

Furnace

Cape Wrath

E 4°W F Dunnet Head Stroma 3°W John o' Groats G

Strathy Point

Loch Eriboll

Ben Hope 927m

HIGHLANDS

Thurso
Halkirk
Wick
River Thurso
Lybster

961m ▲ Ben Klibreck

Loch nan Clar

Kinbrace
Morven ▲ 705m

998m ▲ Ben More Assynt

847m Canisp

Loch Shin

River Helmsdale

Helmsdale

North Sea

Lairg

Brora

Beinn Dearg 1081m ▲

Bonar Bridge
Dornoch
Tarbat Ness

Dornoch Firth

Tain

58

2°W H

1109m ▲ Sgurr Mór

1046m ▲ Ben Wyvis

Invergordon

Cromarty Firth Cromarty Moray Firth

Branderburgh Portknockie Portsoy Banff Rosehearty Fraserburgh
Lossiemouth Buckie Cullen Macduff
Burghead Fochabers
Elgin R. Spey

ND

River Meig

Dingwall

Nairn
Forres

Aberchirder Turriff

River Deveron

Peterhead
Buchan Ness

2

Inverness

R. Beauly

Rothes
Keith
Charlestown of Aberlour

Huntly

Loch Ilardoch

Drumnadrochit

River Nairn

Dufftown

rn Eige 83m

Loch Ness

Invermoriston

Grantown-on-Spey

MORAY

River Spey

Oldmeldrum
Ellon

River Don

Inverurie

ABERDEENSHIRE

River Don

Dyce
ABERDEEN CITY
Aberdeen

Fort Augustus
Invergarry

Aviemore

MONADHLIATH MOUNTAINS

CAIRNGORMS

1244m Cairn Gorm

Aboyne

Banchory

River Dee

57

Loch Lochy

Kingussie
Newtonmore

Ballater

Stonehaven

Ben Alder 1148m ▲

Braemar

1155m ▲ Lochnagar

River North Esk

William 1344m ▲ Ben Nevis

Loch Ericht

GRAMPIAN MOUNTAINS

PERTH

Laurencekirk

Inverbervie

ANGUS

Milton Ness

Blackwater Reservoir

AND

River Isla

Brechin
River South Esk

Montrose

Loch Rannoch

KINROSS

Pitlochry

Kirriemuir

Arbroath

1

Ben Lawers 1214m ▲

River Tay
Aberfeldy

Blairgowrie Rattray
Alyth

Forfar

SIDLAW HILLS

Carnoustie

Loch Tay

Coupar Angus

DUNDEE CITY
Dundee

Tyndrum

Crianlarich

Ben More 1174m ▲

Crieff
River Earn

Perth

Firth of Tay

Dalmally

Loch Earn

Auchterarder

Newburgh
Cupar

St Andrews

SCOTLAND

Loch Katrine

Callander

OCHIL HILLS

Auchtermuchty

Crail

ND BUTE

veraray

Tarbet

Ben Lomond 974m ▲ STIRLING

Dunblane

CLACKMANNAN-SHIRE

Kinross

Loch Leven

FIFE

Glenrothes

Anstruther

Loch Lomond

5°W

River Forth Stirling
Alloa

E 4°W F Kirkcaldy 3°W G

Buckhaven

2°W H

Transverse Mercator Projection
© Oxford University Press

Key

- ▪▪▪ international boundary
- ▪ ▪ national boundary
- ▪ ▪ county or region boundary
- ▬▬ motorway and main roads
- ┼ railway
- ⊕ main airport
- river
- ┼ canal
- lake
- ▲ peak or highest point

towns

- built-up areas
- ■ largest towns
- ● large towns
- · other towns

Land height
measured above sea level

- more than 1000m
- 500-1000m
- 200-500m
- 100-200m
- less than 100m

Transverse Mercator Projection
© Oxford University Press

Scale

10 km

One centimetre on the map measures 10 kilometres on the ground.

one cm

0   10   20   30   40 km

North Sea

Irish Sea

Ben More 1174m
Loch Earn
Crieff
River Earn
Perth
Newburgh
4°W
3°W
St Andrews
Loch Katrine
Auchterarder
Cupar
Callander
Auchtermuchty
Crail
Ben Lomond 974m
Kinross
FIFE
Anstruther
STIRLING
Dunblane
CLACKMANNAN-SHIRE
Loch Leven
Glenrothes
River Forth
Loch Lomond
Alloa
Buckhaven
lochhead
Stirling
Dunfermline
Kirkcaldy
North Berwick
WEST DUNBARTONSHIRE
Falkirk
Grangemouth
Inverkeithing
Firth of Forth
Dunbar
H
56°N
2°W
nsburgh
CAMPSIE FELLS
FALKIRK
Bo'ness
Alexandria
EAST DUNBARTONSHIRE
Falkirk
Linlithgow
Edinburgh
Musselburgh
EAST LOTHIAN
St Abb's Head
North Sea
enock
Dumbarton
Cumbernauld
CITY OF EDINBURGH
Eyemouth
sgow
Clydebank
Kirkintilloch
Bathgate
Livingston
LAMMERMUIR HILLS
Port
Bearsden
Airdrie
WEST LOTHIAN
MIDLOTHIAN
Duns
Whiteadder Water
Berwick-upon-Tweed
Paisley
Coatbridge
Penicuik
River Tweed
Holy Island
RCLYDE
Glasgow
GLASGOW CITY
NORTH LANARKSHIRE
Coldstream
Johnstone
Hamilton
Motherwell
PENTLAND HILLS
Bamburgh
NFREWSHIRE
Wishaw
S
Peebles
Leader Water
Galashiels
Kelso
Wooler
Itcoats
EAST RENFREWSHIRE
East Kilbride
Innerleithen
Melrose
ne
Kilmarnock
R. Clyde
Lanark
O
SCOTTISH BORDERS
815m The Cheviot
River Aln
Alnwick
Darvel
SOUTH LANARKSHIRE
Biggar
T
Broad Law 840m
Selkirk
L
River Tweed
Yarrow Water
Jedburgh
oon
EAST AYRSHIRE
L
St Mary's Loch
BORDERS
Amble
stwick
River Ayr
A
Hawick
River Teviot
River Coquet
Ayr
Cumnock
N
Moffat
River Esk
602m Peel Fell
CHEVIOT HILLS
NORTHUMBERLAND
New Cumnock
Daer Reservoir
D
Ashington
River Doon
Sanquhar
LOWTHER HILLS
River Nith
Kielder Water
River Wansbeck
Blyth
Maybole
Thornhill
River Annan
River Esk
Liddel Water
River Rede
River Blyth
Whitley Bay
SOUTH AYRSHIRE
Loch Doon
Langholm
Cramlington
R. Stinchar
DUMFRIES AND GALLOWAY
Lockerbie
Newcastle upon Tyne
55°N
R. Cree
St John's Town of Dalry
Lochmaben
River Annan
Gateshead
Sout Shield
Newton Stewart
New Galloway
Dumfries
Annan
River Irthing
Haltwhistle
Hexham
River Tyne
Washington
Sunderland
nluce
Castle Douglas
Loch Ken
Brampton
River Derwent
Consett
Chester-le-Street
Wigtown
Dalbeattie
Kirkbean
Carlisle
Cross Fell 893m
River Wear
Durham
enluce
Gatehouse of Fleet
River Dee
Wigton
M6
River Eden
P
DURHAM
Spennymoor
Whithorn
Kirkcudbright
Solway Firth
E
Bishop Auckland
Wigtown Bay
Maryport
River Ellen
790m Mickle Fell
River Tees
Newton Aycliffe
Workington
R. Derwent
Cockermouth
Skiddaw 931m
Penrith
N
Barnard Castle
DARLINGTON
Whitehaven
Keswick
Derwent Water
Appleby-in-Westmorland
Brough
Darlington
St Bees Head
CUMBRIA
Ullswater
N
Richmond
Irish Sea
Point of Ayre
Helvellyn 950m
Kirkby Stephen
River Swale
Scafell Pike 978m
LAKE DISTRICT
ENGLAND
Leyburn
Seascale
Ambleside
I
NORTH YORKSHIRE
Snaefell 620m
Ramsey
Windermere
Windermere
River Ure
Kirk Michael
Coniston Water
River Wharfe
Peel
Kendal
River Greta
Whernside 737m
704m Great Whernside
Ripon
South Barrule 483m
ISLE OF MAN
Whernside
Ingleborough 723m
693m Pen-y-Ghent
R. Nidd
Douglas
Dalton-in-Furness
Carnforth
Lune
River Wharfe
River Aire
Castletown
Barrow-in-Furness
Morecambe Bay
Lancaster
560m Ward's Stone
54°N
Morecambe
Heysham
M6
FOREST OF BOWLAND
Skipton
Ilkley
Barnoldswick

Irish Sea

Luce Bay
Wigtown Bay
Wigtown
Newton Stewart
Glenluce
Whithorn
Drummore
Mull of Galloway

Gatehouse of Fleet
Castle Douglas
Dalbeattie
Kirkcudbright
Kirkbean
R. Dee

Lochmaben
Langholm
Lockerbie
Annan
Solway Firth

Carlisle
River Irthing
Brampton
Haltwhistle
Hexham
R. Tyne

NORTHUMBERLAND
Cramlington
Newcastle upon Tyne
Gateshead
Washington
Chester-le-Street
Consett
Durham
R. Wansbeck

Point of Ayre
Ramsey
Kirk Michael
Snaefell 620m
Peel
South Barrule 483m
Douglas
ISLE OF MAN
Castletown

Maryport
Workington
Whitehaven
St Bees Head
Seascale
R. Derwent
Cockermouth
Wigton
River Ellen

931m
Skiddaw
Keswick
Derwent Water
Helvellyn 950m
978m
Scafell Pike
Windermere
Coniston Water
Ambleside
Windermere

CUMBRIA
Penrith
LAKE DISTRICT
Ullswater
River Eden

Cross Fell 893m
Mickle Fell 790m
Appleby-in-Westmorland
Brough
Kirkby Stephen

PENNINES
DURHAM
Bishop Auckland
Newton Aycliffe
Spennymoor
Barnard Castle
DARLINGTON
Darlington
River Wear
River Tees
River Derwent

Carmel Head
Amlwch
Holyhead
Holy Island
ISLE OF ANGLESEY
Anglesey
Bangor
Bethesda
Caernarfon
Caernarfon Bay
Snowdon 1085m
GWYNEDD
LLEYN PENINSULA
Portmadog
Pwllheli
Harlech
Barmouth
Dolgellau
Cader Idris 892m
Cardigan Bay

Dalton-in-Furness
Barrow-in-Furness
Morecambe Bay
Morecambe
Heysham
Carnforth
Lancaster
Ward's Stone 560m
River Lune

Whernside 737m
R. Greta
Ingleborough 723m
Pen-y-Ghent 693m
Great Whernside 704m
River Wharfe
River Swale
Leyburn
Richmond
NORTH YORKSHIRE
R. Ure
River Nidd
Rip

Fleetwood
River Wyre
BLACKPOOL
Blackpool
Lytham St Anne's
Preston
LANCASHIRE
River Ribble
Leyland
Southport
Formby
Skelmersdale
Kirkby
Bootle
MERSEYSIDE
Wallasey
Birkenhead
Liverpool
Widnes
St Helens
Wigan
Chorley
Blackburn
BLACKBURN WITH DARWEN
Bolton
Bury
GREATER MANCHESTER
Salford
Manchester
Sale
Warrington
WARRINGTON
Runcorn
HALTON
Ellesmere Port

FOREST OF BOWLAND
Barnoldswick
Nelson
Burnley
Ilkley
Keighley
Bradford
Halifax
Brighouse
Huddersfield
Dewsbu
WEST YORKSHIRE
Rochdale
Oldham
Stockport
Cheadle
The Peak 636m
Macclesfield
Buxton
Bakewell
DERBYSH
Matlock
Lees
Lee
River Aire
Skipton
Harrogat

Llandudno
Conwy
Rhyl
Colwyn Bay
Flint
FLINTSHIRE
Denbigh
Mold
River Dee
R. Conwy
River Clwyd
CONWY
DENBIGHSHIRE
Blaenau Ffestiniog
Bala
Bala Lake
Lake Vyrnwy
CAMBRIAN MOUNTAINS
POWYS
R. Vyrnwy
Welshpool
Machynlleth
R. Dyfi
R. Severn
Montgomery

Chester
Northwich
Winsford
CHESHIRE
Crewe
Wrexham
WREXHAM
Llangollen
River Dee
Oswestry
Whitchurch
Market Drayton
Newport
TELFORD AND WREKIN
Telford 407m
The Wrekin
Shrewsbury
SHROPSHIRE
Kidsgrove
STOKE-ON-TRENT
Newcastle-under-Lyme
Stoke-on-Trent
ENGLAND
Stafford
STAFFORDSHIRE
Cannock
Rugeley
Lichfield
Tamworth
Burton upon Trent
Uttoxeter
Ashbour
Wolverhampton
Walsall
DERBY
River Dove
River Derwent
Newport

Transverse Mercator Projection
© Oxford University Press

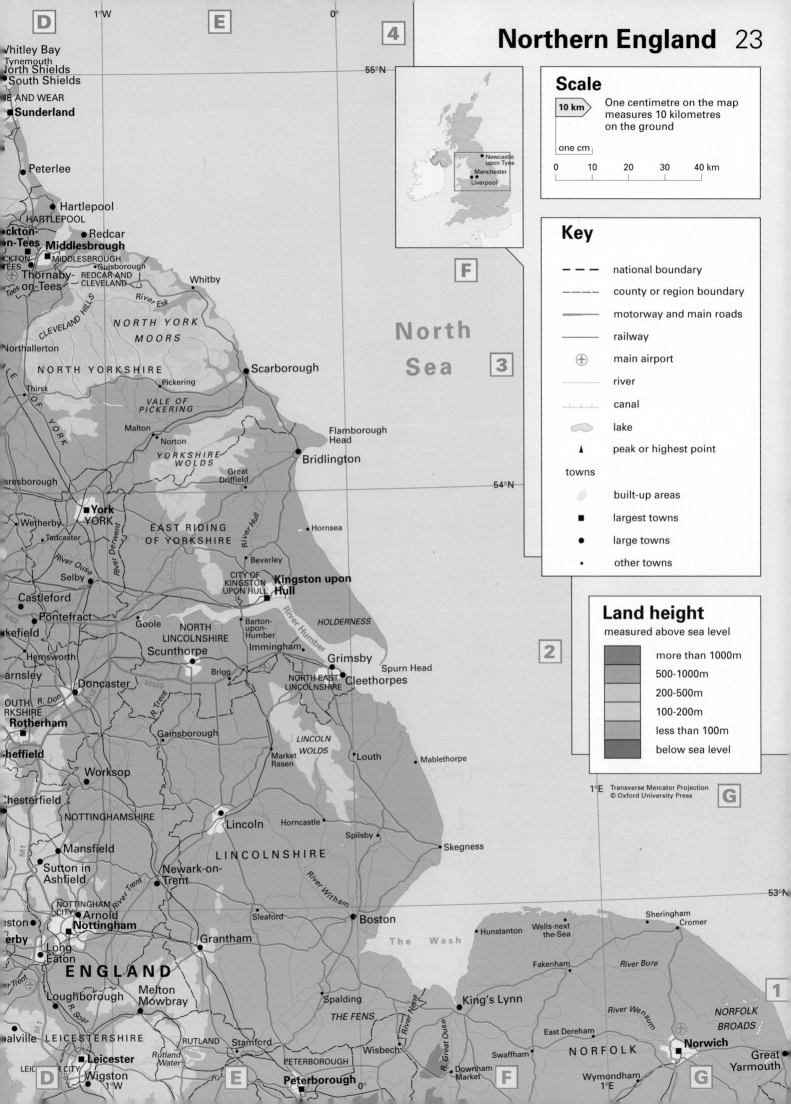

NORTHERN

Formby

A 6°W

B 5°W

C

D 4°W

MERSEYSIDE

Irish Sea

Bootle
Wallasey
Liverpool
Birkenhead

words
Malahide

Howth

Amlwch

Carmel Head

Llandudno Rhyl

River Dee

M53

Dublin
Dún Laoghaire

Holyhead

ISLE OF
ANGLESEY

Conwy Colwyn
Bay

FLINTSHIRE

3

Holy
Island

Anglesey

Bangor

R. Conwy

Denbigh

River Clwyd

Flint

Mold

Bray

Bethesda

Greystones

Caernarfon

Snowdon
1085m ▲

CONWY

DENBIGHSHIRE

**REPUBLIC OF
IRELAND**

Caernarfon
Bay

Wrexham

WREXF

53°N
Wicklow

Blaenau
Ffestiniog

River Dee

Llangollen

Porthmadog

Bala

LLEYN PENINSULA

Pwllheli

Bala
Lake

Oswestry

Harlech

GWYNEDD

Lake
Vyrnwy

Irish
Sea

905m ▲
Aran Fawddy

R. Vyrnwy

Barmouth

Dolgellau

Welshpool

Cader Idris ▲
892m

Arklow

Machynlleth

R. Dyfi

WALES

Montgom

Cardigan
Bay

R. Severn

2

Newtown

752m ▲
Plynlimon

SHROPS

Aberystwyth

Llanidloes

CEREDIGION

Rhayader

Knighton

Aberaeron

New Quay

Llandrindod
Wells

King

St George's Channel

River Teifi

POWYS

Cemaes Head

Lampeter

Builth Wells

Strumble Head

Cardigan

River Teifi

MYNYDD
EPPYNT

R. Wye

Hay-on-W

52°N

Newcastle Emlyn

Llandovery

Fishguard

CAMBRIAN

BLACK

MYNYDD
PRESELI

CARMARTHENSHIRE

R. Tywi

River Usk

Brecon

811m ▲

MOUNTAIN

St David's Head

St David's PEMBROKESHIRE

Carmarthen

Llandeilo

BRECON
▲ 886m
BEACONS

Abergavenny

Haverfordwest

R. Tywi

Ammanford

Merthyr
Tydfil

Ebbw Vale

St Brides
Bay

Kidwelly

Milford
Haven

Burry
Port

Pontardulais

Aberdare

BLAENAU
GWENT

TORFA

MERTHYR
TYDFIL

Abertillery

NEATH
PORT TALBOT

RHONDDA

Pontypool

Carmarthen
Bay

SWANSEA

Neath

CYNON

Cwmbran

1

Pembroke

Tenby

Llanelli

Rhondda

TAFF

CAERPHILLY

Worms Head

GOWER

Pontypridd

Caerphilly

Newport

Swansea

Port
Talbot

BRIDGEND

CARDIFF

NEWPC

Bridgend

THE VALE OF
GLAMORGAN

Cardiff

ATLANTIC

Barry

OCEAN

Bristol Channel

Weston-super-
Mare

Bridgwater
Bay

Lundy

Ilfracombe

Lynton

Minehead

Transverse Mercator Projection
© Oxford University Press

B

C 5°W

DEVON EXMOOR

Dunkery
Beacon
519m ▲

D

SOMERSET

6°W

4°W

3°

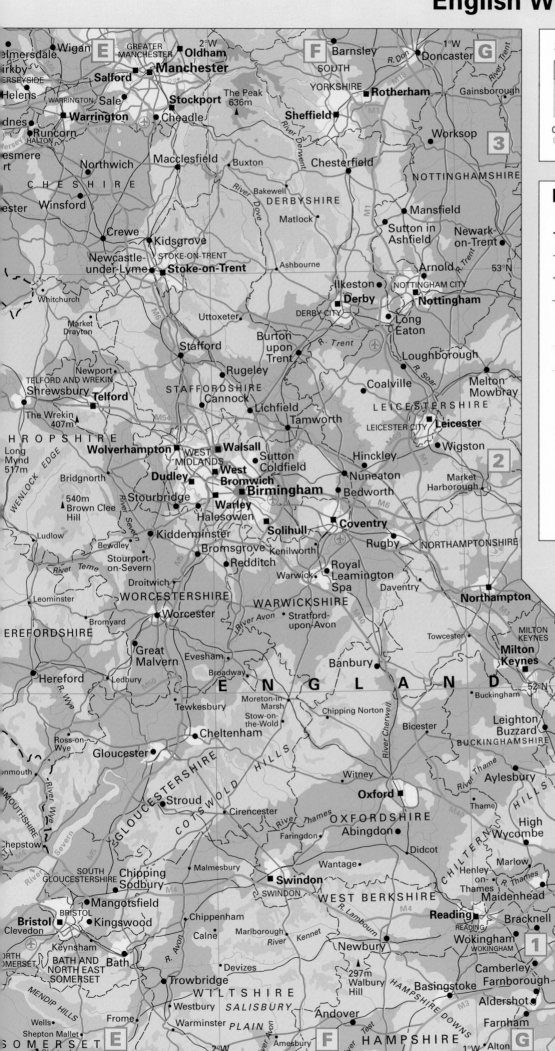
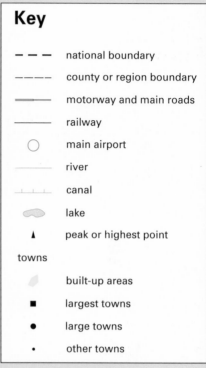

Transverse Mercator Projection
© Oxford University Press

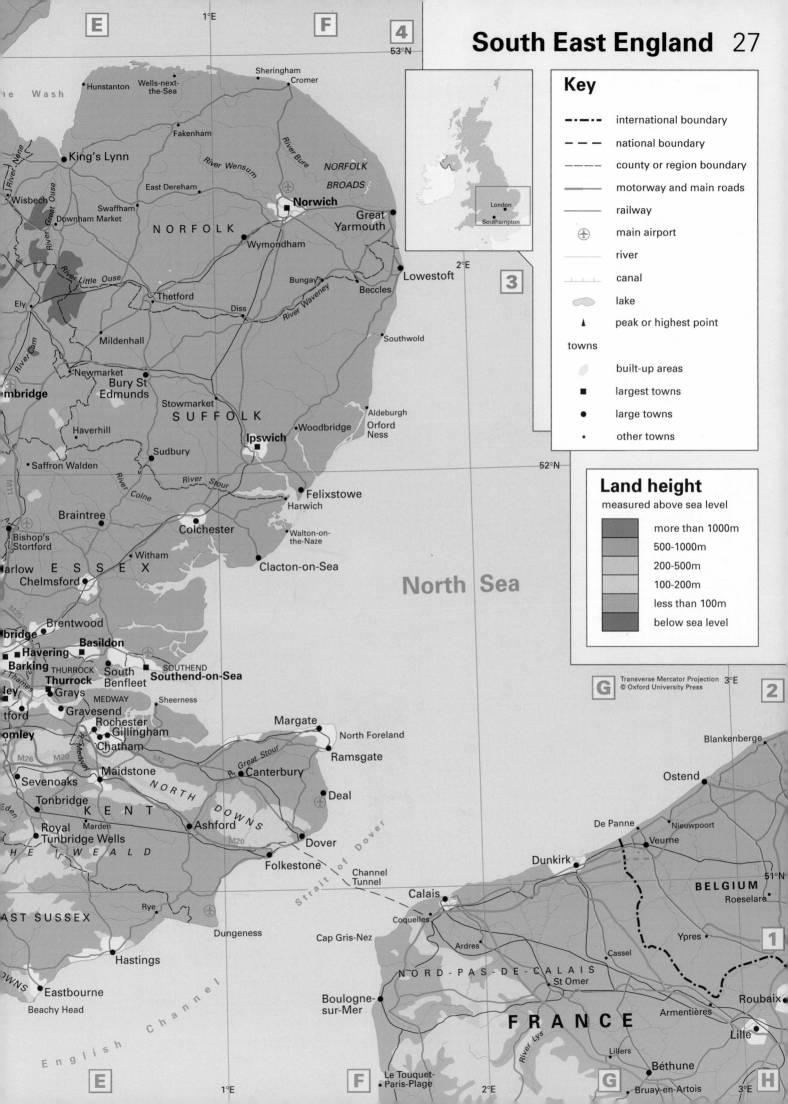

28 South West England

Scale

10 km > One centimetre on the map measures 10 kilometres on the ground.

one cm
0 10 20 30 40 km

Key

—··—··— international boundary
— — — national boundary
- - - - county or region boundary
━━━ motorway and main roads
——— railway
⊕ main airport
——— river
—|—|— canal
🌫 lake
▲ peak or highest point

towns
🌫 built-up areas
■ largest towns
● large towns
· other towns

Land height
measured above sea level

more than 1000m
500-1000m
200-500m
100-200m
less than 100m

4°W
C
D
Bridg
THE VAL
GLAMOR

Bristol Channe

ATLANTIC
5°W
B
OCEAN

Lynton
Ilfracombe
Minehead
Dunkery Beac
▲ 519m
River Exe
Braunton
Barnstaple
EXMOOR
Bideford Bay
South
Molton

51°N
Hartland
Point
Bideford
River Taw
DEVON
Tiverton
Cullomp
Great
Torrington
River Torridge
Crediton
Bude
Bay
Bude
Holsworthy
Hatherleigh
Okehampton
Exeter
Boscastle
Yes Tor
River
619
Exm
Launceston
DARTMOOR
Teign
Brown Willy
▲ 420m
River Tavy
Dawlish
BODMIN
Bovey Tracey
Teignmouth
MOOR
R. Tamar
Tavistock
Newton Abbot
Trevose Head
Padstow
Buckfastleigh
Torba
Wadebridge
River Camel
TORBAY
River Fowey
Newquay
Bodmin
Liskeard
PLYMOUTH
Totnes
Bri
CORNWALL
Lostwithiel
Saltash
Fowey
Torpoint
Dartmouth
St Agnes
St
Plymouth
Looe
Austell
Fal
Kingsbridge
Truro
Bigbury
Start
Redruth
River
Bay
Bay
St Ives
Camborne
Salcombe
Start Point
Penryn
St Just
Falmouth
Penzance
Sennen
Helston
Land's
End
Mount's Bay
Mullion

50°N
A
6°W
Lizard
Lizard
St Martin's
Point
Bryher Tresco
St Mary's
Hugh Town
Isles of
Scilly

ATLANTIC

OCEAN

49°N

1
A
Transverse Mercator Projection
© Oxford University Press
B
5°W
C
4°W
D

Cardiff
Mangotsfield
Clevedon
BRISTOL
Bristol
Kingswood
Chippenham
Weston-super-Mare
NORTH SOMERSET
Keynsham
BATH AND NORTH EAST SOMERSET
Bath
Calne
Devizes
Trowbridge
WILTSHIRE
M4
297m Walbury Hill
Camberley
Farnborough
Basingstoke
Woking
Epsom
SURREY
dgwater Bay
MENDIP HILLS
Wells
Shepton Mallet
Glastonbury
Frome
Westbury
Warminster
SALISBURY
PLAIN
Andover
HAMPSHIRE DOWNS
Aldershot
Farnham
Guildford
Dorking
Bridgwater
QUANTOCK HILLS
Amesbury
River Test
Stockbridge
R. Itchen
Winchester
Alton
Petersfield
Haslemere
NORTH DOWNS
51°N
Taunton
SOMERSET
River Tone
River Yeo
Wincanton
Mere
Salisbury
Shaftesbury
HAMPSHIRE
Romsey
Eastleigh
River Meon
Waterlooville
Havant
SOUTH DOWNS
R. Arun
Horsham
WEST SUSSEX
Vellington
M5
Ilchester
Sherborne
Yeovil
Totton
Southampton
SOUTHAMPTON
Fareham
Gosport
M27
PORTSMOUTH
Chichester
Arundel
Worthing
Ilminster
Crewkerne
Chard
River Axe
Blandford Forum
Wimborne Minster
Ringwood
River Avon
Fawley
M27
Portsmouth
Bognor Regis
Littlehampton
Honiton
Axminster
DORSET
River Stour
POOLE
BOURNEMOUTH
Lymington
Cowes
Ryde
Selsey Bill
Bridport
Lyme Regis
River Frome
Poole
Christchurch
Bournemouth
Newport
ISLE OF WIGHT
Sandown
Shanklin
Sidmouth
Seaton
Lyme Bay
Dorchester
Wareham
The Needles
Weymouth
Swanage
St Alban's Head
St Catherine's Point
Portland Bill

English Channel

50°N

Cap de la Hague
Auderville
Alderney
Barfleur
Baie de la Seine
Cherbourg
Guernsey
St Peter-Port
Sark
CHANNEL
Valognes
FRANCE
ISLANDS
Carteret
Jersey
St Helier
Carentan
Isigny-sur-Mer
Lessay
St-Lô
River Vire
Caen
Coutainville
Coutances
River Orne
49°N

3°W   2°W   1°W

Most people in the United Kingdom live in large towns or cities.

Total number of people, 1991

England	48 million
Scotland	5 million
Wales	3 million
N. Ireland	2 million
U.K.	**58 million**

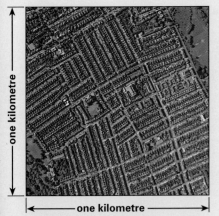

More than 250 people live in this square kilometre.

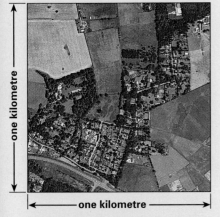

About 100 people live in this square kilometre.

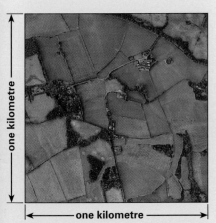

Fewer than 50 people live in this square kilometre.

Transverse Mercator Projection
© Oxford University Press

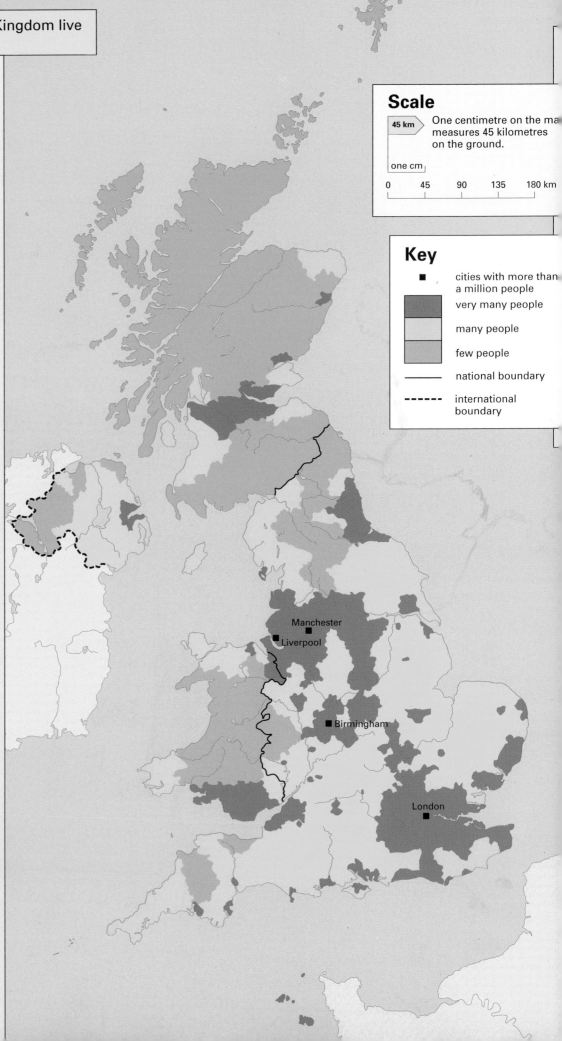

Scale

45 km

One centimetre on the map measures 45 kilometres on the ground.

one cm

0	45	90	135	180 km

Key

■ cities with more than a million people

very many people

many people

few people

—— national boundary

- - - international boundary

Manchester
Liverpool
Birmingham
London

Scale

45 km One centimetre on the map measures 45 kilometres on the ground.

one cm

| 0 | 45 | 90 | 135 | 180 km |

Farmers produce food by growing crops and keeping animals.

Key

	mostly livestock farms	cattle are kept for meat
	mostly hill farms	sheep are kept for meat and wool
	mostly dairy farms	cows are kept for milk
	mostly arable farms	crops are grown

Many farms in Britain are mixed farms. Farmers grow crops *and* keep animals.

🌲 forestry trees are planted for wood

✳ market gardening fruit and vegetables are grown

no farming built-up areas

Transverse Mercator Projection
© Oxford University Press

More people work in offices
than in factories in the
United Kingdom.

Scale

45 km ▷ One centimetre on the map
measures 45 kilometres
on the ground.

one cm |

0   45   90   135   180 km

Key

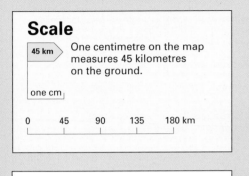 major industrial area

• office and business centre

—— national boundary

------ international boundary

Jobs change

Over time some industries
close down.
People lose their jobs.

New industries are often
based on high technology
but not everyone can find work.

Central
Lowlands

City of
Glasgow

City of
Edinburgh

City of
Newcastle

Tyneside

City of
Belfast

City of
Leeds

Greater
Manchester

West Yorkshire

Merseyside

City of
Manchester

South Yorkshire

East
Midlands

City of
Birmingham

West
Midlands

South
Wales

Greater
London

City of London

City of
Cardiff

City of Bristol

City of Croydon

City of Southampton

Transverse Mercator Projec
© Oxford University P

Coal, oil, and natural gas hold
energy which originally came
from the sun.

Scale

60 km

One centimetre on the map
measures 60 kilometres
on the ground.

one cm

0	60	120	180	240 km	

Oil and gas fields
have drilling and
pumping rigs

Key

• largest coal mines

—⊢— gas field and pipeline

—⊢— oil field and pipeline

largest power stations

▲ burning coal, oil or gas

▲ using water power

▲ using nuclear power

△ using wind power

△ wind generator

Magnus

Tern
Statfjord
Brent
Ninian
North Alwyn

Foinaven

Bruce
Frigg
Beryl

Birch
Claymore
Piper
Scott

Forties

Fulmar

Kilmorack
Affric
Glenmoriston
Peterhead

Tummel
Cruachan
Breadalbane
Sloy
Longannet
Longannet
Torness
Hunterston
Cockenzie

Ballylumford

Ellington
Blyth Harbour

Hartlepool
Teesside

Heysham
South
Morecambe
Coal
Clough
Riccall
Whitemoor
Wistow
Drax
Ferrybridge
Eggborough
Ravenspurn
West Sole
Harworth
West Burton
Cottam
Pickerill
Thoresby
Indefatigable
Dinorwig
Fiddler's
Ferry
Ratcliffe-on-Soar
Hewett
Leman
Mynydd
Cemmaes
Ashfordby
Penrhyddlan
Llidiartywaun
Daw Mill
Sizewell

Tower
Didcot
Tilbury
Grain
Aberthaw
Kingsnorth
Hinkley

Delabole
Carland Cross
Wytch
Farm

Electricity is made in power stations

Thermal power stations
burn coal, oil, or gas to make
steam which drives turbines.
Nuclear power stations use the
heat from a nuclear reaction.
Hydro electric power stations use
water power.
Wind power stations use
wind generators.

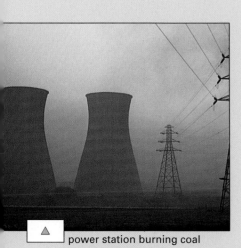

△ power station burning coal

Transverse Mercator Projection
© Oxford University Press

Roads and railways do not always take the shortest route between places.

Scale

45 km

One centimetre on the map measures 45 kilometres on the ground.

one cm

| 0 | 45 | 90 | 135 | 180 km |

Key

— major road
— motorway
— main railway
• road or rail terminal
built-up areas
land over 200 metres
land below 200 metres
— national boundary

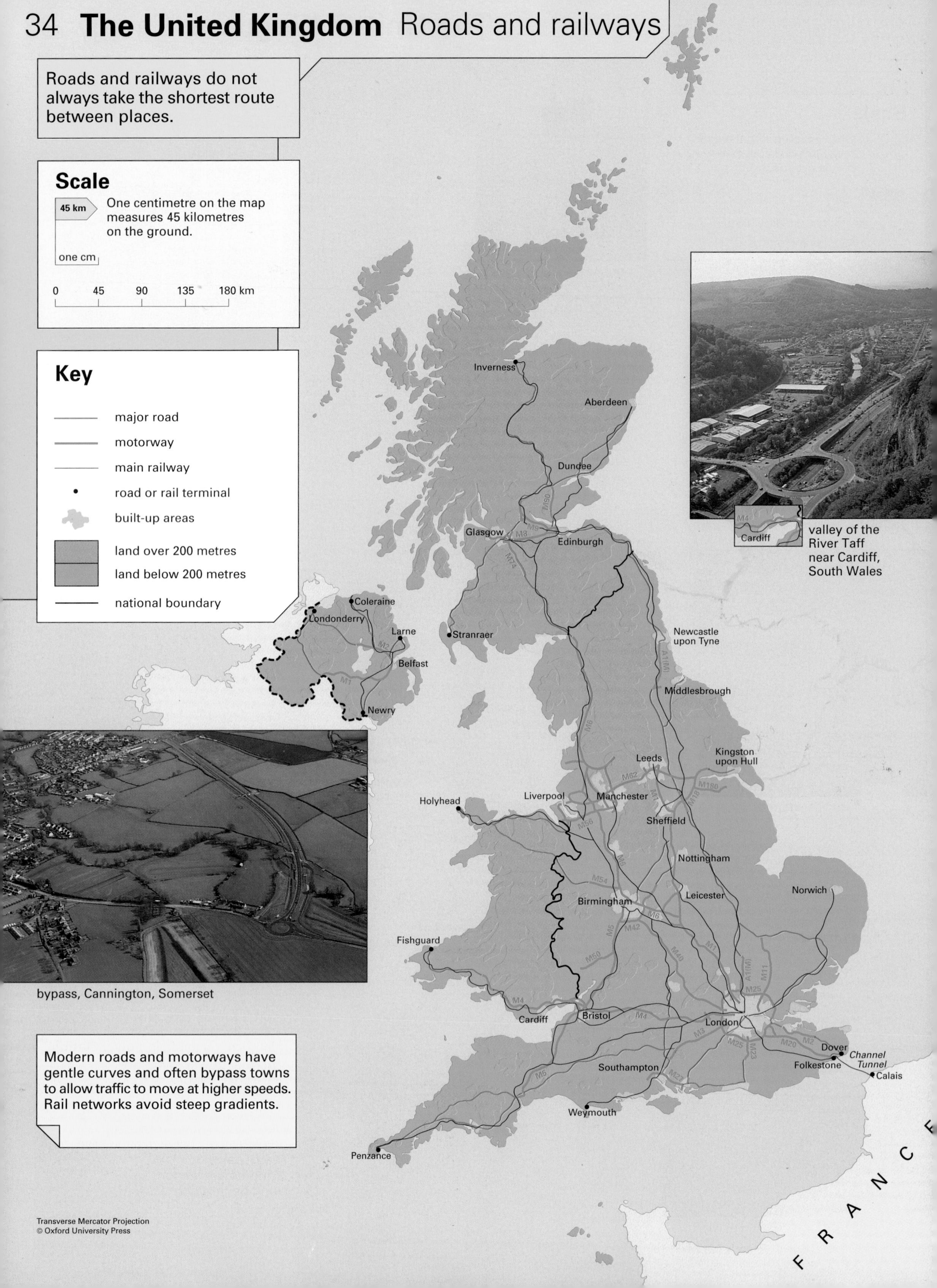

valley of the River Taff near Cardiff, South Wales

bypass, Cannington, Somerset

Modern roads and motorways have gentle curves and often bypass towns to allow traffic to move at higher speeds. Rail networks avoid steep gradients.

Inverness
Aberdeen
Dundee
Glasgow
Edinburgh
M90
M9
M8
M74
Coleraine
Londonderry
Larne
M2
Belfast
Stranraer
M1
Newry
Newcastle upon Tyne
A1(M)
Middlesbrough
Kingston upon Hull
Leeds
M62
M180
Holyhead
Liverpool
Manchester
M1
Sheffield
M56
Nottingham
M6
Leicester
Norwich
Fishguard
M54
Birmingham
M42
M5
M6
A1(M)
M1
M50
M40
M5
Cardiff
Bristol
M4
London
M25
M4
M11
M3
Southampton
M23
M27
M20
M2
Dover
Folkestone
Channel Tunnel
Calais
Weymouth
Penzance
Cardiff
M4

F R A N C E

Transverse Mercator Projection
© Oxford University Press

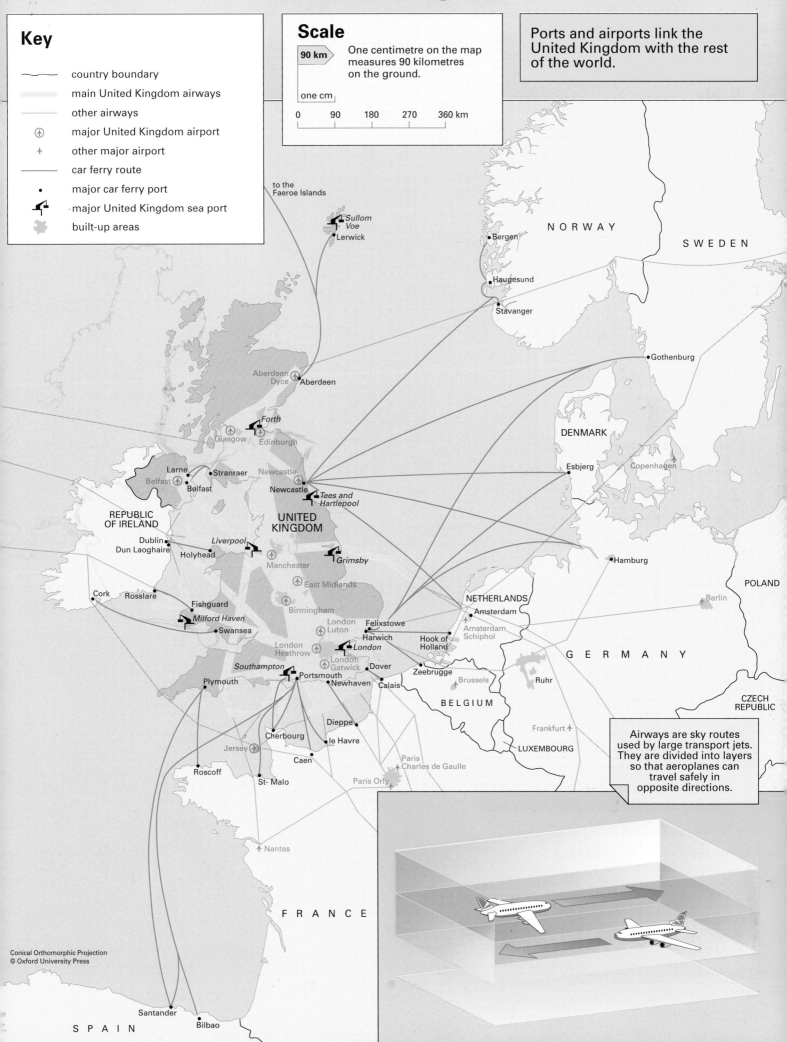

Key

⎯⎯⎯	country boundary
▒▒▒	main United Kingdom airways
⎯⎯	other airways
✈	major United Kingdom airport
✈	other major airport
⎯⎯	car ferry route
•	major car ferry port
⚓	major United Kingdom sea port
▨	built-up areas

Scale

90 km ⟶ One centimetre on the map measures 90 kilometres on the ground.

one cm

0   90   180   270   360 km

Ports and airports link the United Kingdom with the rest of the world.

Airways are sky routes used by large transport jets. They are divided into layers so that aeroplanes can travel safely in opposite directions.

to the Faeroe Islands

Sullom Voe
Lerwick

NORWAY
SWEDEN

Bergen

Haugesund
Stavanger

Gothenburg

Aberdeen Dyce • Aberdeen

DENMARK

Forth
Glasgow
Edinburgh

Esbjerg
Copenhagen

Larne
Belfast
Belfast
Stranraer

Newcastle
Newcastle
Tees and Hartlepool

REPUBLIC OF IRELAND

UNITED KINGDOM

Hamburg

POLAND
Berlin

Dublin
Dun Laoghaire
Holyhead

Liverpool
Manchester

Grimsby

East Midlands

Cork
Rosslare

Fishguard

Birmingham

NETHERLANDS
Amsterdam
Amsterdam Schiphol

GERMANY

Milford Haven
Swansea

London Luton

Felixstowe
Harwich
Hook of Holland

Ruhr

CZECH REPUBLIC

London Heathrow

London
London Gatwick

Dover

Zeebrugge
Brussels

Plymouth

Southampton
Portsmouth
Newhaven
Calais

BELGIUM

Dieppe

Cherbourg
le Havre

Frankfurt

LUXEMBOURG

Jersey

Caen

Paris Charles de Gaulle

Roscoff

St- Malo

Paris Orly

Nantes

FRANCE

Santander
Bilbao

SPAIN

Damage to our land, sea, and air is called pollution.

Scale

45 km — One centimetre on the map measures 45 kilometres on the ground.

one cm

| 0 | 45 | 90 | 135 | 180 km |

Key

- built-up areas
- most polluted rivers and estuaries
- most polluted coasts and beaches

areas affected by acid rain

- heavy pollution
- moderate pollution
- light pollution

How to fight pollution

Poisonous gases from cars and factories

Poisonous waste in rivers from factories and farms

Loud noise from aircraft, factories and traffic

Dumping raw sewage in the sea

Leaving litter

STOP

ATLANTIC OCEAN

North Sea

Irish Sea

Loch Fyne

Firth of Forth

River Clyde

R. Lagan

R. Bann

R. Tyne

R. Aire

R. Ribble

River Mersey

R. Aire

R. Don

R. Humber

River Trent

R. Nene

R. Avon

R. Severn

R. Thames

Bristol Channel

English Channel

Transverse Mercator Projection
© Oxford University Press

The United Kingdom Conservation

Protecting nature, resources, and buildings is called conservation.

Scale

45 km
One centimetre on the map measures 45 kilometres on the ground.

one cm

0   45   90   135   180 km

Key

National Parks

areas of outstanding scenery and beauty

protected coast

★ World Heritage Sites

major built-up areas

National Park
Snowdonia

Area of outstanding scenery and beauty
Countryside in the Cotswold

Protected coast
The Dorset coast at Durdle Door

★
World Heritage Site
Stonehenge

★ St Kilda

South Lewis, Harris and North Uist

Wester Ross

Cairngorm Mountains

Aberdeen

Ben Nevis and

Dundee

Jura

Loch Lomond

Edinburgh

Glasgow

Upper Tweeddale

Giant's Causeway

Antrim Coast and Glens

Sperrin

Belfast

Mourne

Northumberland

Hadrian's Wall

Newcastle upon Tyne

North Pennines

Durham Castle/Cathedral

Middlesbrough

Lake District

Yorkshire Dales

North York Moors

Nidderdale

Forest of Bowland

Fountain's Abbey/Studley Royal Park

Leeds

Kingston upon Hull

Liverpool

Manchester

Sheffield

Anglesey

Clwydian Range

Peak District

Lincolnshire Wolds

Castles/Town Walls of King Edward

LLeyn

Snowdonia

Nottingham

Leicester

Birmingham

Norfolk Coast

Norwich

The Broads Authority

Ironbridge Gorge

Shropshire Hills

Pembrokeshire Coast

Wye Valley

Blenheim Palace

Cotswolds

Suffolk Coast and Heaths

Brecon Beacons

Gower

Cardiff

Bristol

North Wessex Downs

Chilterns

London

Westminster Palace/Abbey

Bath

Surrey Hills

Kent Downs

Exmoor

Stonehenge/Avebury

High Weald

Blackdown Hills

Cranbourne Chase

Southampton

Sussex Downs

Dorset

New Forest

Bodmin Moor

Dartmoor

Isle of Wight

Transverse Mercator Projection
Oxford University Press

Europe is the smallest continent but is the most crowded.

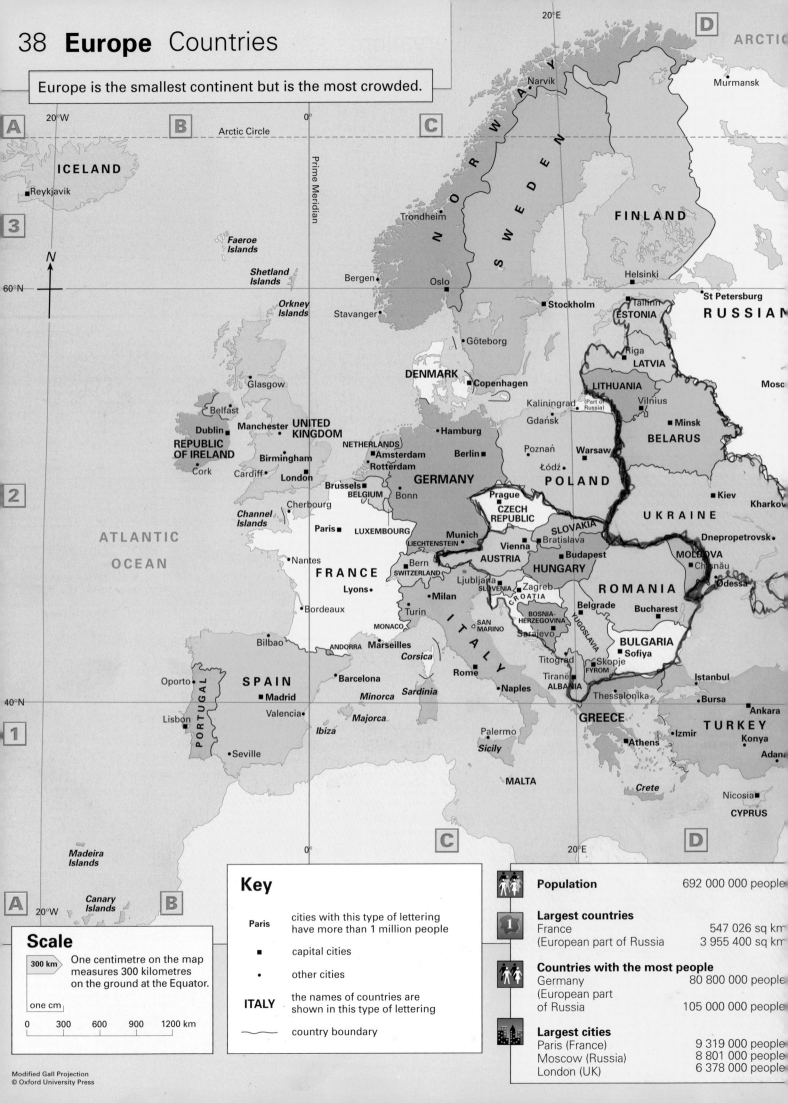

ARCTIC

Key

Paris   cities with this type of lettering have more than 1 million people

■   capital cities

•   other cities

ITALY   the names of countries are shown in this type of lettering

——   country boundary

Scale

300 km ▷ One centimetre on the map measures 300 kilometres on the ground at the Equator.

one cm ⊢⊣

0   300   600   900   1200 km

Modified Gall Projection
© Oxford University Press

Population	692 000 000 people
Largest countries France (European part of Russia	547 026 sq km 3 955 400 sq km
Countries with the most people Germany (European part of Russia	80 800 000 people 105 000 000 people
Largest cities Paris (France) Moscow (Russia) London (UK)	9 319 000 people 8 801 000 people 6 378 000 people

E 60°E F

OCEAN

Arctic Circle 3

60°N

EDERATION (RUSSIA)

• Perm

• Nizhniy Novgorod

• Kazan

• Ufa

• Samara

2

• Volgograd

netsk

• Rostov-on-Don

GEORGIA Tbilisi ■

TURKEY

40°N

1

40°E

E

Modified Gall Projection
© Oxford University Press

The European Union

20°W 0° 20°E 40°E

Arctic Circle

Prime Meridian

60°N 60°N

40°N 40°N

20°W 0° 20°E 40°E

The European Union

The European Union is a group of countries which have agreed to work together and share the same plans for industry, agriculture, transport, and trade.

Key

— country boundary

countries which are members of the European Union

countries which have applied to be members of the European Union

other European countries

Scale for both small maps

650 km

One centimetre on the map measures 650 kilometres on the ground at the Equator.

one cm

0 650 1300 1950 2600 km

How big is Europe?

See how long journeys within Europe take, by air ✈ and by rail 🚄

20°W 0° 20°E 40°E

Prime Meridian

Arctic Circle

60°N 60°N

Moscow

London 3.5 hours Berlin 35.5 hours

1 hour

Paris

15 hours 3.4 hours

Rome

40°N 40°N

Athens

20°W 0° 20°E

Europe is a continent of peninsulas and islands.

A 20°W
B Arctic Circle 0°
C
D 20°E North Cape ARCTIC

3
Iceland
1491m△ Mount Hekla
Faeroe Islands
Shetland Islands
Lofoten Islands
Kola Peninsu
Wh Se

SCANDINAVIAN HIGHLANDS
2469m△ Galdhøpiggen
R. Glomma
Lak One
Lake Ladoga

N

60°N
Outer Hebrides
Orkney Islands
Ben Nevis △1344m
North Sea
Lake Vänern
Gotland
Baltic Sea
Lake Peipus
Bornholm

2
ATLANTIC OCEAN
Ireland
Great Britain
R. Thames
English Channel
Channel Islands
Friesian Islands
River Elbe
River Rhine
River Seine
River Danube
NORTH EUROPEAN PLAIN
River Vistula
River Dniester
Pripet Marshes
River Dnieper

River Loire
Bay of Biscay
MASSIF CENTRAL
4807m Mont Blanc
R. Rhône
ALPS
River Po
CARPATHIANS
River Danube

PYRENEES
River Ebro
River Duero
MESETA
River Tagus
Corsica
Balearic Islands
Minorca
Sardinia
APPENNINES
Adriatic Sea
Black Se
2917m△ Mount Olympus
ANATOLIA PLATEAU
TAURUS MOUNTA
s

1
40°N
Majorca
Ibiza
Tyrrhenian Sea
Ionian Sea
Aegean Sea

Mediterranean Sea
Sicily
3323m△ Mount Etna
Malta
Peloponnese
Crete
Cyprus

A 20°W
B Strait of Gibraltar
Prime Meridian 0°
C
D 20°E

Key

Colours show the height of the land.

- more than 2000 metres
- 1000 – 2000 metres
- 500 – 1000 metres
- 200 – 500 metres
- less than 200 metres
- this land is below the level of the sea
- ▲ peak or highest point
- river
- lake
- marsh
- ice cap

Scale

300 km   One centimetre on the map measures 300 kilometres on the ground.

one cm

0   300   600   900   1200 km

Area		10 498 000 sq km
Highest peak		
Mount Elbrus		5 642 m
Mont Blanc		4 807 m
Lowest point		
Caspian Sea		28 m below sea level
Largest freshwater lake		
Ladoga		18 390 sq km
Longest river		
Volga		3 688 km

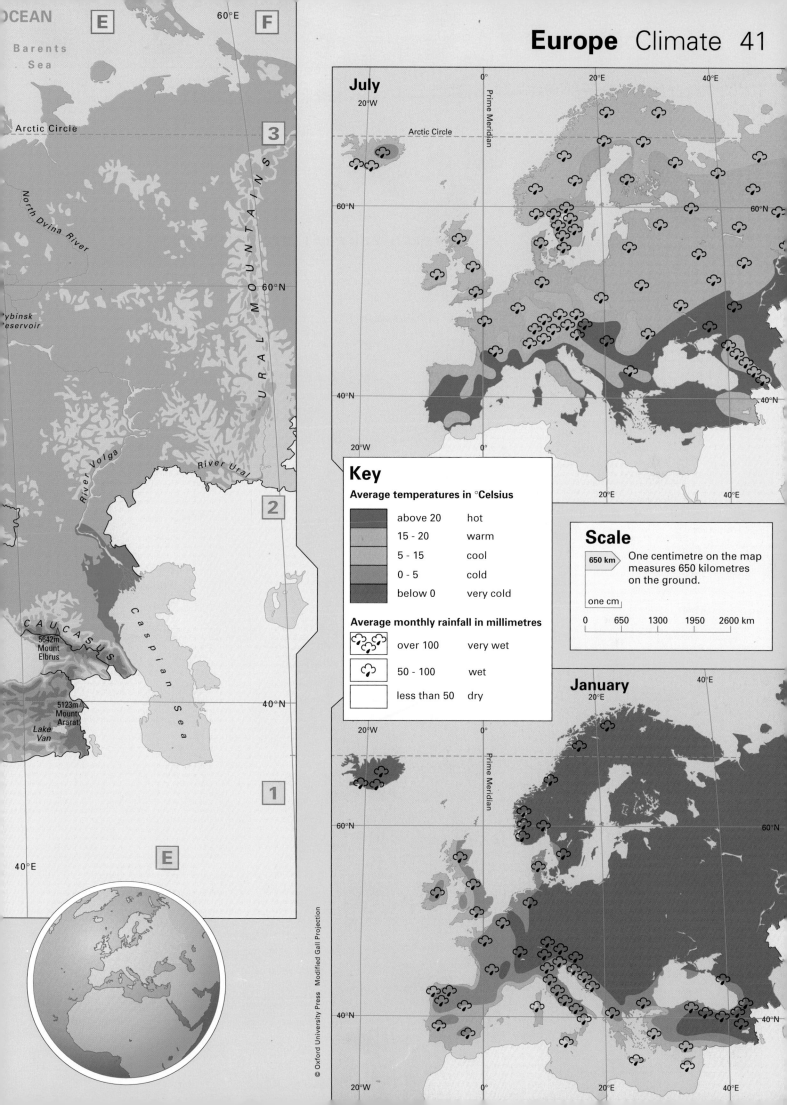

OCEAN

Barents
Sea

E   60°E   F

3

Arctic Circle

North Dvina River

60°N

URAL MOUNTAINS

60°N

ybinsk
eservoir

2

River Volga   River Ural

C A U C A S U S
5642m
Mount
Elbrus

Caspian Sea

40°N

5123m
Mount
Ararat
Lake
Van

1

40°E   E

40°N

July

20°W   0°   20°E   40°E
Prime Meridian

Arctic Circle

60°N   60°N

40°N   40°N

20°W   0°   20°E   40°E

Key

Average temperatures in °Celsius

above 20	hot
15 - 20	warm
5 - 15	cool
0 - 5	cold
below 0	very cold

Average monthly rainfall in millimetres

⛈⛈	over 100	very wet
☁	50 - 100	wet
	less than 50	dry

Scale

650 km   One centimetre on the map
measures 650 kilometres
on the ground.

one cm

0   650   1300   1950   2600 km

January

40°E
20°E

20°W   0°   Prime Meridian

Arctic Circle

60°N   60°N

40°N   40°N

20°W   0°   20°E   40°E

© Oxford University Press   Modified Gall Projection

Of all the continents, Asia has the greatest variety of landscapes and people.

RUSSIAN FEDERATION (RUSSIA)

Yakutsk

St Petersburg
Moscow
Nizhniy Novgorod
Perm
Kazan
Ufa
Samara
Yekaterinburg
Chelyabinsk
Omsk
Novosibirsk

Volgograd
Rostov-on-Don
Gur'yev
Akmola
KAZAKHSTAN
Ulan Bator
MONGOLIA
Harbin
Changchun
Jilin
Shenyang
Fushun
Jinzhou
Anshan
Yingkou
Dandong
NORTH KOREA
Sapp

ARMENIA
Yerevan
Baku
AZERBAIJAN
Tashkent
UZBEKISTAN
Bishkek
KIRGYZSTAN
Beijing
Tianjin
Taiyuan
Zibo
Dalian
Seoul
SOUTH KOREA
Pyongyang
JAPAN
Nagoya
Tokyo
Yokohama

Aleppo
SYRIA
Beirut
LEBANON
Damascus
Tabriz
TURKMENISTAN
Ashkhabad
TAJIKISTAN
Dushanbe
Mashhad
AFGHANISTAN
JAMMU AND KASHMIR
Qingdao
Lanzhou
Jinan
Xi'an
Osaka
Kita-Kyushu

ISRAEL
Amman
Jerusalem
JORDAN
Baghdad
IRAQ
Tehran
IRAN
Esfahan
Kabul
Islamabad
Lahore
CHINA
Chengdu
Nanjing
Wuhan
Shanghai
Hangzhou

Basra
KUWAIT
Kuwait City
Bushehr
BAHRAIN
QATAR
PAKISTAN
Delhi
NEPAL
Kathmandu
Kanpur
Chongqing
Nanchang
Wenzhou

Riyadh
Doha
Abu Dhabi
Karachi
BHUTAN
Thimpu
BANGLADESH
Dhaka
Chittagong
Guangzhou
Taipei
Tropic of Cancer

Jiddah
SAUDI ARABIA
UNITED ARAB EMIRATES
Muscat
Ahmadabad
Calcutta
MYANMAR
Hanoi
Hong Kong
TAIWAN
Kao-hsiung

OMAN
INDIA
Mumbai (Bombay)
Hyderabad
Rangoon
Vientiane
LAOS
VIETNAM
THAILAND

San'a
YEMEN REPUBLIC
Bangalore
Chennai (Madras)
Bangkok
CAMBODIA
Manila
Quezon
PHILIPPINES

SRI LANKA
Phnom Penh
Ho Chi Minh City

Bangalore
Colombo

MALDIVES
MALAYSIA
BRUNEI DARUSSALAM
Bandar Seri Begawan

Medan
Kuala Lumpur
SINGAPORE

Palembang
Equator

Jakarta
Bandung
Semarang
Surabaya
INDONESIA

INDIAN OCEAN

Tropic of Capricorn

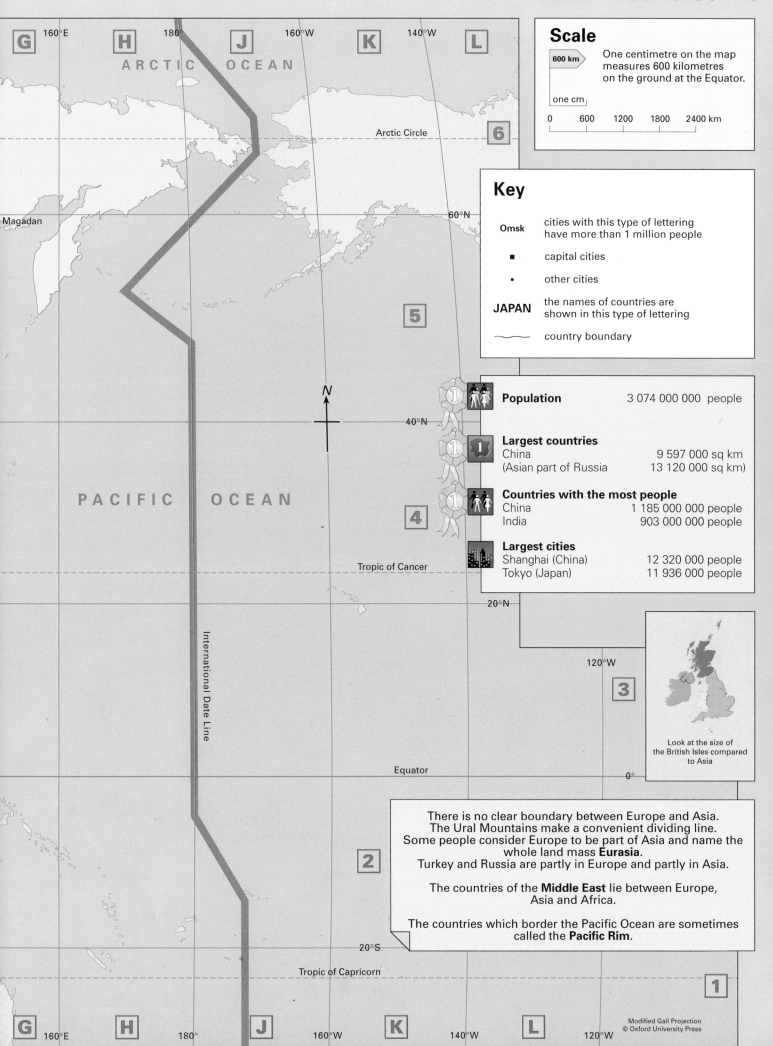

G 160°E   H 180°   J   160°W   K   140°W   L

ARCTIC OCEAN

Arctic Circle

6

Magadan

60°N

N

40°N

PACIFIC OCEAN

Tropic of Cancer

5

4

International Date Line

20°N

120°W

3

Look at the size of
the British Isles compared
to Asia

Equator

0°

20°S

Tropic of Capricorn

2

1

G 160°E   H 180°   J   160°W   K   140°W   L   120°W

Scale

600 km

One centimetre on the map
measures 600 kilometres
on the ground at the Equator.

one cm

0   600   1200   1800   2400 km

Key

Omsk   cities with this type of lettering
have more than 1 million people

■   capital cities

•   other cities

JAPAN   the names of countries are
shown in this type of lettering

‿‿   country boundary

Population   3 074 000 000 people

Largest countries
China   9 597 000 sq km
(Asian part of Russia   13 120 000 sq km)

Countries with the most people
China   1 185 000 000 people
India   903 000 000 people

Largest cities
Shanghai (China)   12 320 000 people
Tokyo (Japan)   11 936 000 people

There is no clear boundary between Europe and Asia.
The Ural Mountains make a convenient dividing line.
Some people consider Europe to be part of Asia and name the
whole land mass **Eurasia**.
Turkey and Russia are partly in Europe and partly in Asia.

The countries of the **Middle East** lie between Europe,
Asia and Africa.

The countries which border the Pacific Ocean are sometimes
called the **Pacific Rim**.

Modified Gall Projection
© Oxford University Press

Asia covers one third of the land surface of the Earth.

20°E A 40°E B 60°E C 80°E D 100°E E 120°E F 140°E

Barents Sea

CENTRAL SIBERIAN PLATEAU

Arctic Circle

SIBERIAN LOWLAND

Lake Onega

Lake Ladoga

URAL MOUNTAINS

River Ob

River Lena

60°N

Angara River

River Volga

River Irtysh

ALTAI MOUNTAINS

Lake Baykal

River Amur

Sea of Okhot

5

Aral Sea

Lake Balkhash

Gobi Desert

Hokkaido

Black Sea

CAUCASUS

Caspian Sea

5642m Mount Elbrus

40°N

5123m Mount Ararat

Mount Demavend △ 5671m

Communism Peak ▽ 7495m △

KUNLUN SHAN

Hwang-Ho River

Sea of Japan

Korean Peninsula

Honshu

Yellow Sea

Shikoku Kyushu

R. Euphrates

R. Tigris

ZAGROS MOUNTAINS

HINDU KUSH

River Indus

8611m k2

TIBETAN PLATEAU

Red Basin

Yangtze River

East China Sea

4

d Sea n below level

Arabia Peninsula

The Gulf

Mount Everest 8848m

HIMALAYAS

Ryukyu Islands

Tropic of Cancer

Red Sea

Thar Desert

River Ganges

Brahmaputra R.

Irrawaddy River

Salween River

20°N

Mouths of the Ganges

Arabian Sea

WESTERN GHATS

DECCAN

Bay of Bengal

South China Sea

Luzon

Socotra

Andaman Islands

Mekong River

Mindoro

3

Andaman Sea

Gulf of Thailand

Mindanao

Nicobar Islands

Mount Kinabalu 4101m △

Maldive Archipelago

Malay Peninsula

Borneo

Equator 0°

Sumatra

Sulawesi

5030m △ Jaya Peak

New Guinea

Java Sea

Java

Arafura Sea

INDIAN OCEAN

Bali

Timor Sea

2

20°S

1

Tropic of Capricorn

A 40°E B 60°E C 80°E D 100°E E 120°E F 140°E

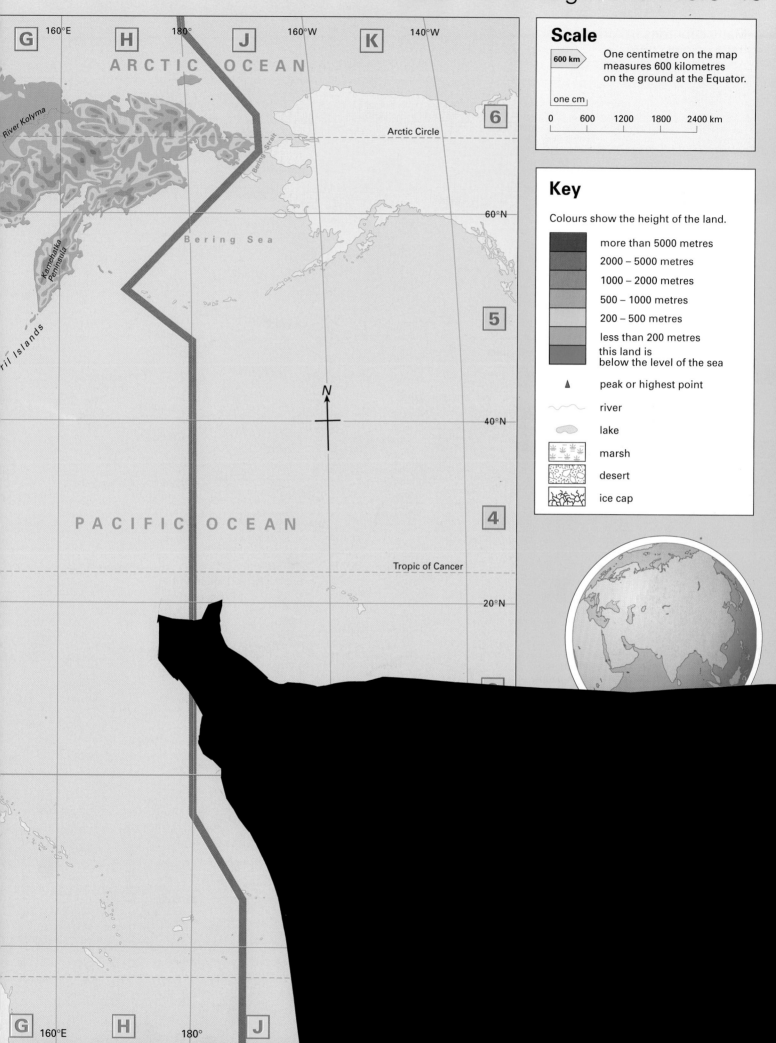

ARCTIC OCEAN

River Kolyma

6

Arctic Circle

60°N

Bering Sea

Kamchatka
Peninsula

5

ril Islands

N

40°N

PACIFIC OCEAN

4

Tropic of Cancer

20°N

G 160°E   H 180°   J

Scale

600 km

One centimetre on the map
measures 600 kilometres
on the ground at the Equator.

one cm

0   600   1200   1800   2400 km

Key

Colours show the height of the land.

more than 5000 metres

2000 – 5000 metres

1000 – 2000 metres

500 – 1000 metres

200 – 500 metres

less than 200 metres

this land is
below the level of the sea

▲   peak or highest point

~~~   river

◯   lake

marsh

desert

ice cap

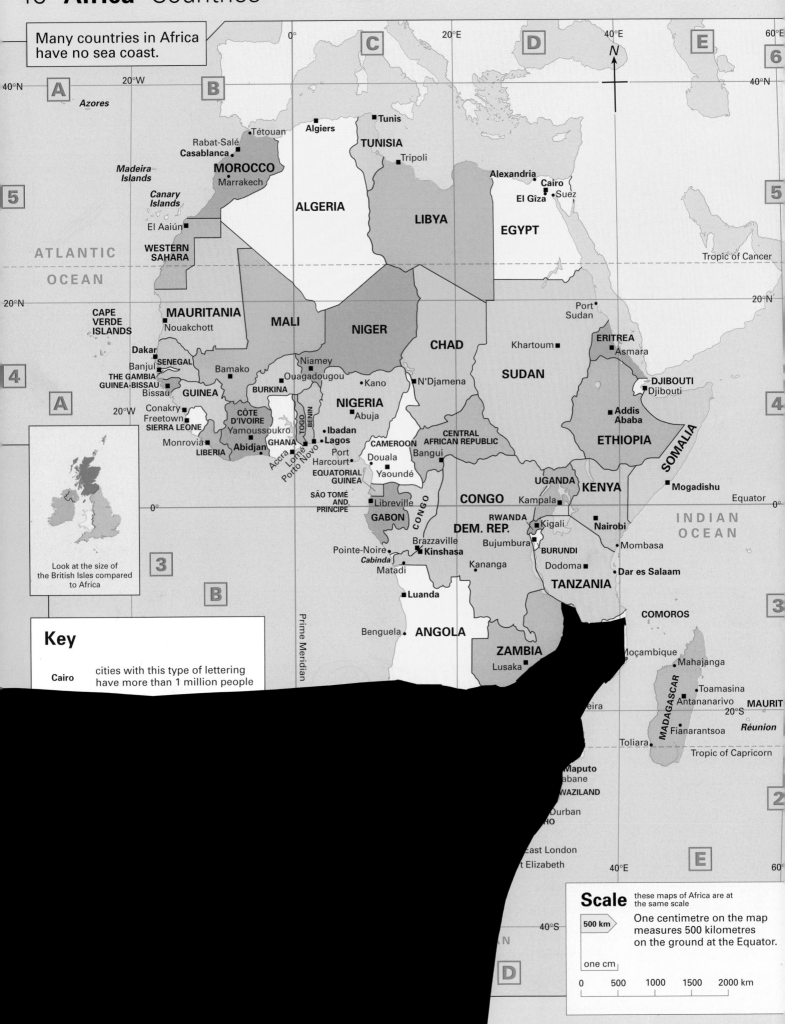

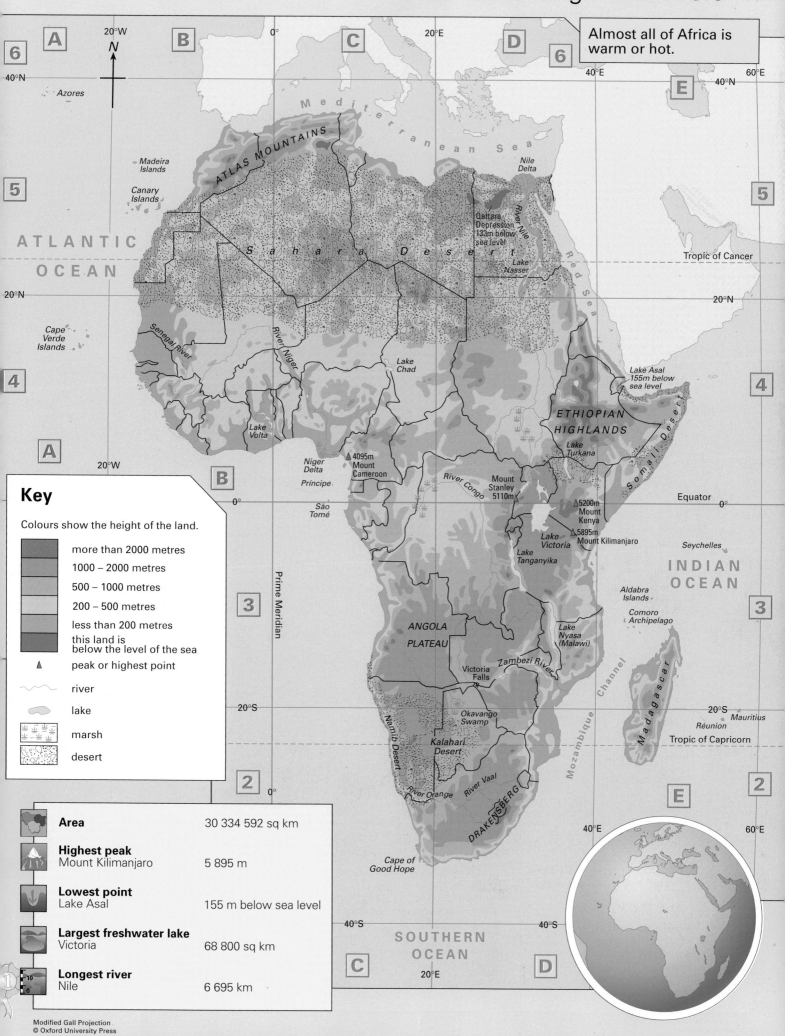

Almost all of Africa is warm or hot.

Key

Colours show the height of the land.

- more than 2000 metres
- 1000 – 2000 metres
- 500 – 1000 metres
- 200 – 500 metres
- less than 200 metres
- this land is below the level of the sea
- ▲ peak or highest point
- ∿ river
- ⬭ lake
- marsh
- desert

Area	30 334 592 sq km	
Highest peak Mount Kilimanjaro	5 895 m	
Lowest point Lake Asal	155 m below sea level	
Largest freshwater lake Victoria	68 800 sq km	
Longest river Nile	6 695 km	

Modified Gall Projection
© Oxford University Press

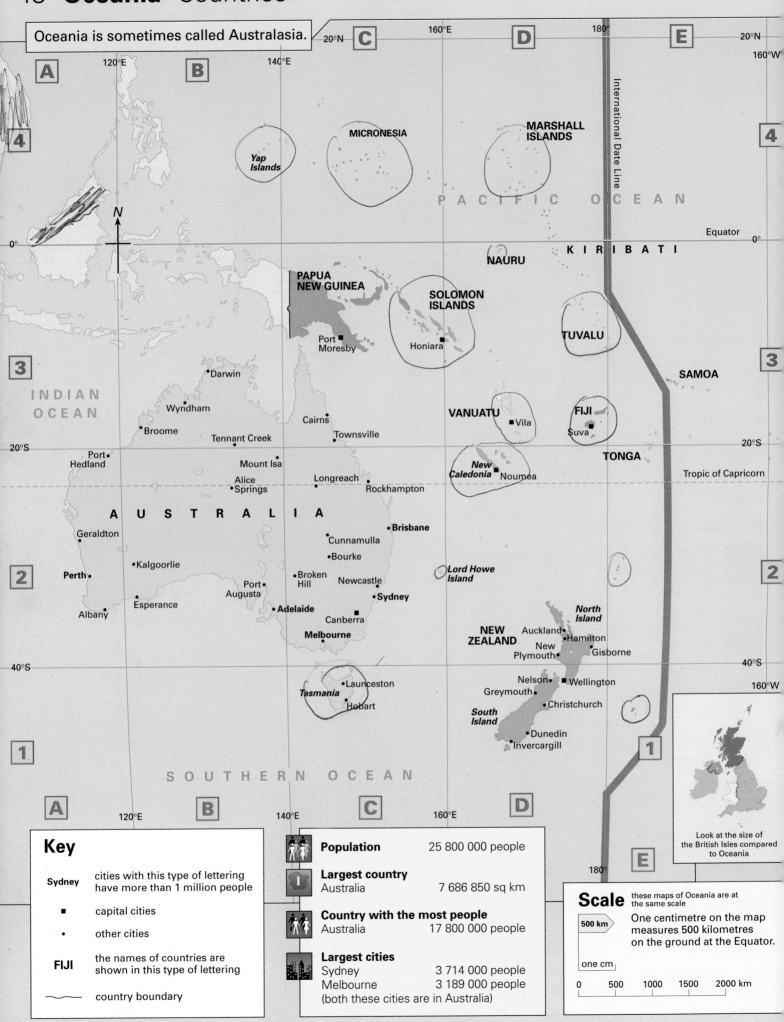

Oceania is sometimes called Australasia.

A   120°E   B   140°E   C   20°N   160°E   D   180°   E   20°N

160°W

MICRONESIA

MARSHALL ISLANDS

Yap Islands

P A C I F I C   O C E A N

Equator   0°

NAURU   K I R I B A T I

PAPUA NEW GUINEA

SOLOMON ISLANDS

Port Moresby

Honiara

TUVALU

SAMOA

INDIAN OCEAN

•Darwin

Wyndham•

•Broome

Port• Hedland

VANUATU   ■Vila   **FIJI**   Suva■

TONGA

Tropic of Capricorn

•Cairns

Townsville•

Tennant Creek•

Mount Isa•

Alice •Springs   •Longreach   Rockhampton•

New Caledonia   ■ Noumea

20°S

A U S T R A L I A

Geraldton•

•Cunnamulla

•Bourke

•Brisbane

•Broken Hill   Newcastle•

•Kalgoorlie

Perth•

Port• Augusta

•Esperance

Albany•

•Sydney

Adelaide•

Canberra■

Melbourne•

Lord Howe Island

North Island

Auckland•

NEW ZEALAND   New Plymouth•   Hamilton•

Gisborne•

Nelson•   ■Wellington

Greymouth•

•Christchurch

Tasmania   •Launceston

Hobart•

South Island

•Dunedin

Invercargill•

40°S   160°W

S O U T H E R N   O C E A N

A   120°E   B   140°E   C   160°E   D

180°   E

Key

Sydney   cities with this type of lettering have more than 1 million people

■   capital cities

•   other cities

FIJI   the names of countries are shown in this type of lettering

‿‿‿   country boundary

Modified Gall Projection
© Oxford University Press

Population   25 800 000 people

Largest country
Australia   7 686 850 sq km

Country with the most people
Australia   17 800 000 people

Largest cities
Sydney   3 714 000 people
Melbourne   3 189 000 people
(both these cities are in Australia)

Look at the size of the British Isles compared to Oceania

Scale   these maps of Oceania are at the same scale

500 km   One centimetre on the map measures 500 kilometres on the ground at the Equator.

one cm

0   500   1000   1500   2000 km

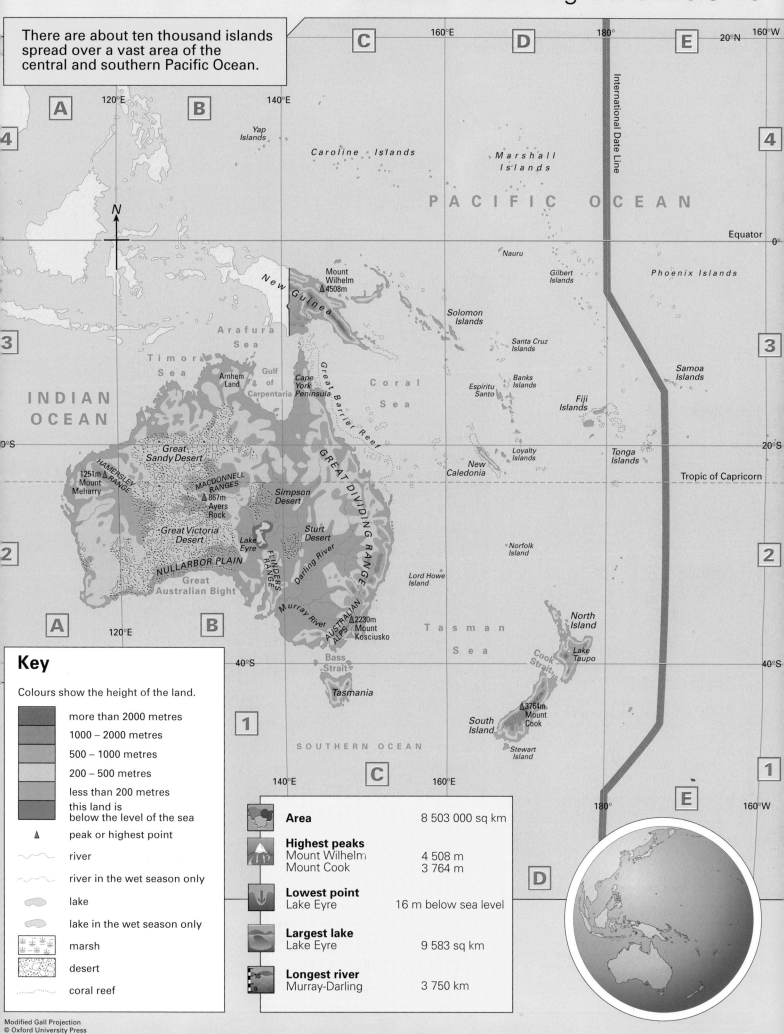

There are about ten thousand islands spread over a vast area of the central and southern Pacific Ocean.

PACIFIC OCEAN

Caroline Islands

Marshall Islands

Yap Islands

International Date Line

Equator

Nauru

Gilbert Islands

Phoenix Islands

Mount Wilhelm △4508m

New Guinea

Arafura Sea

Solomon Islands

Santa Cruz Islands

Samoa Islands

Timor Sea

Arnhem Land

Gulf of Carpentaria

Cape York Peninsula

Great Barrier Reef

Coral Sea

Espiritu Santo

Banks Islands

Fiji Islands

INDIAN OCEAN

Great Sandy Desert

Loyalty Islands

New Caledonia

Tonga Islands

Tropic of Capricorn

1251m △ Mount Meharry

HAMERSLEY RANGE

MACDONNELL RANGES

△ 867m Ayers Rock

Simpson Desert

GREAT DIVIDING RANGE

Great Victoria Desert

NULLARBOR PLAIN

Lake Eyre

FLINDERS RANGE

Sturt Desert

Darling River

Norfolk Island

Lord Howe Island

Great Australian Bight

Murray River

AUSTRALIAN ALPS

△2230m Mount Kosciusko

Tasman Sea

North Island

Lake Taupo

Cook Strait

Bass Strait

Tasmania

South Island

△3764m Mount Cook

Stewart Island

SOUTHERN OCEAN

Key

Colours show the height of the land.

- more than 2000 metres
- 1000 – 2000 metres
- 500 – 1000 metres
- 200 – 500 metres
- less than 200 metres
- this land is below the level of the sea
- ▲ peak or highest point
- river
- river in the wet season only
- lake
- lake in the wet season only
- marsh
- desert
- coral reef

Area		8 503 000 sq km
Highest peaks	Mount Wilhelm	4 508 m
	Mount Cook	3 764 m
Lowest point	Lake Eyre	16 m below sea level
Largest lake	Lake Eyre	9 583 sq km
Longest river	Murray-Darling	3 750 km

North America is dominated by the huge countries of the United States and Canada.

Scale

these maps of North America are at the same scale

600 km

One centimetre on the map measures 600 kilometres on the ground at the Equator.

one cm

| 0 | 600 | 1200 | 1800 | 2400 km |

Key

Miami — cities with this type of lettering have more than 1 million people

■ capital cities

• other cities

CUBA — the names of countries are shown in this type of lettering

⌒ country boundary

Population — 415 778 000 people

Largest countries
Canada — 9 976 140 sq km
United States of America (USA) — 9 372 610 sq km
(The world's longest border is between the United States and Canada.)

Country with the most people
United States of America — 257 000 000 people

Largest cities
Mexico (Mexico) — 15 048 000 people
New York City (USA) — 7 333 253 people

Look at the size of the British Isles compared to North America

Modified Gall Projection
© Oxford University Press

The huge Rocky Mountain range forms the backbone of North America.

Key

Colours show the height of the land.

- more than 2000 metres
- 1000 – 2000 metres
- 500 – 1000 metres
- 200 – 500 metres
- less than 200 metres
- this land is below the level of the sea
- ▲ peak or highest point
- river
- lake
- marsh
- desert
- ice cap

Area		24 241 000 sq km
Highest peak Mount McKinley		6 194 m
Lowest point Death Valley		86 m below sea level
Largest freshwater lake Lake Superior		83 270 sq km
Longest river Mississippi-Missouri		6019 km

Modified Gall Projection
© Oxford University Press

Brazilians speak Portuguese. Most other South Americans speak Spanish.

ATLANTIC OCEAN

N

PACIFIC OCEAN

Tropic of Cancer

20°N

Scale these maps of South America are at the same scale

500 km

One centimetre on the map measures 500 kilometres on the ground at the Equator.

one cm

| 0 | 500 | 1000 | 1500 | 2000 km |

Key

Lima — cities with this type of lettering have more than 1 million people

■ — capital cities

• — other cities

PERU — the names of countries are shown in this type of lettering

⌇ — country boundary

Santa Marta
Barranquilla **Maracaibo** Caracas
Cartagena **Valencia** • Barcelona
VENEZUELA Ciudad Guayana
Ciudad Georgetown Paramaribo
• **Medellín** Bolívar **GUYANA** Cayenne
Buenaventura ■ **Bogotá** **SURINAME** **FRENCH GUIANA**
• **Cali** Boa Oiapoque
COLOMBIA Vista

Aruba *Netherlands Antilles*

0° Equator Quito Macapá

Galapagos Islands **ECUADOR** Belém São Luís
Guayaquil **Manaus** • **Fortaleza**
Iquitos Santarém • Natal
  Teresina • João Pessoa
  Recife
Pucallpa **B R A Z I L**
PERU Pôrto • Aracaju
■ **Lima** Velho **Salvador**
Cuzco
  Cuiabá
Arequipa **BOLIVIA** • **Brasília**
  Santa Goiânia
■ La Paz Cruz
Arica • Sucre Uberaba Belo Horizonte
20°S • Vitória

Tropic of Capricorn **PARAGUAY** Nova Iguaçu Rio de Janeiro
Antofagasta São Paulo
  • Salta Asunción Curitiba
CHILE

Pôrto Alegre ATLANTIC OCEAN

Córdoba
Mendoza **URUGUAY**
Valparaíso **Rosario**
Santiago Buenos Aires Montevideo
Concepción **ARGENTINA**
  Bahía Blanca • Mar del Plata

Juan Fernandez Islands

Look at the size of the British Isles compared to South America

40°S

Puerto Comodoro
Montt Rivadavia

• Stanley
Falkland Islands

Punta Arenas

South Georgia

60°S

Population 283 519 000 people

Largest countries
Brazil 8 511 966 sq km
Argentina 2 776 890 sq km

Country with most people
Brazil 159 100 000 people

Largest cities
Buenos Aires (Argentina) 11 256 000 people
São Paulo (Brazil) 9 627 000 people
Rio de Janeiro (Brazil) 5 473 000 people

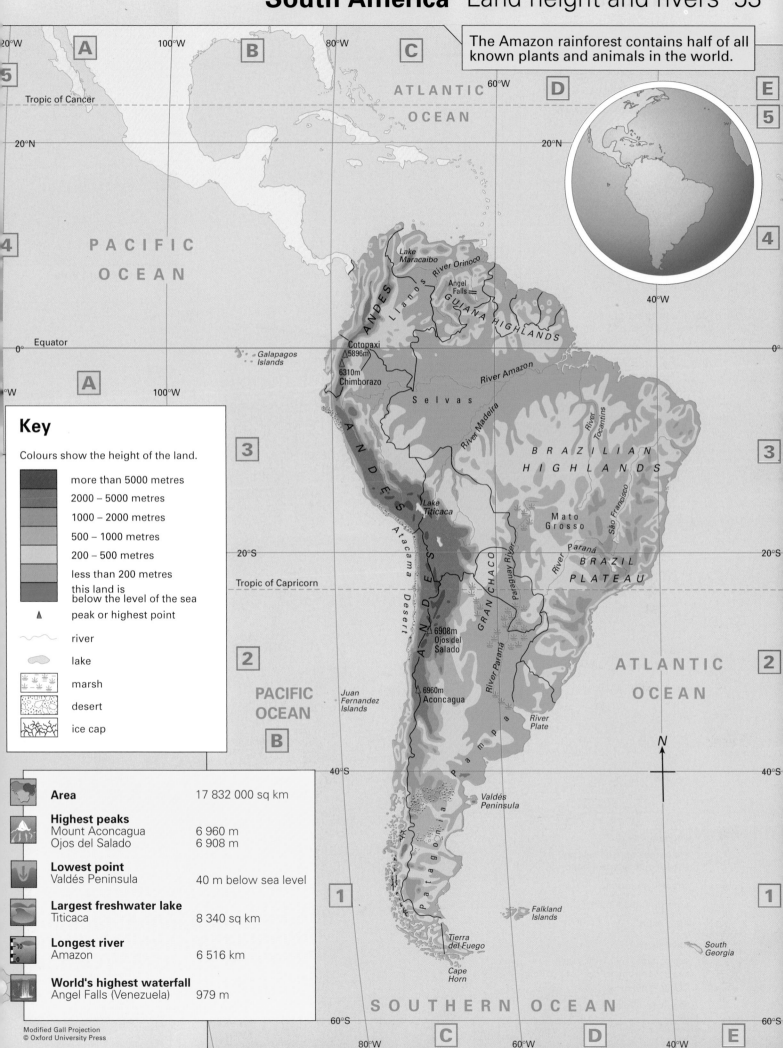

The Amazon rainforest contains half of all known plants and animals in the world.

Key

Colours show the height of the land.

- more than 5000 metres
- 2000 – 5000 metres
- 1000 – 2000 metres
- 500 – 1000 metres
- 200 – 500 metres
- less than 200 metres
- this land is below the level of the sea
- ▲ peak or highest point
- ～ river
- lake
- marsh
- desert
- ice cap

Area   17 832 000 sq km

Highest peaks
Mount Aconcagua   6 960 m
Ojos del Salado   6 908 m

Lowest point
Valdés Peninsula   40 m below sea level

Largest freshwater lake
Titicaca   8 340 sq km

Longest river
Amazon   6 516 km

World's highest waterfall
Angel Falls (Venezuela)   979 m

Tropic of Cancer
20°N
ATLANTIC OCEAN
PACIFIC OCEAN
Equator
Galapagos Islands
Lake Maracaibo
River Orinoco
Angel Falls
GUIANA HIGHLANDS
Llanos
ANDES
Cotopaxi △5896m
△6310m Chimborazo
Selvas
River Amazon
River Madeira
River Tocantins
BRAZILIAN HIGHLANDS
Mato Grosso
São Francisco
Lake Titicaca
Atacama Desert
GRAN CHACO
Paraguay River
River Paraná
BRAZIL PLATEAU
Tropic of Capricorn
20°S
△6908m Ojos del Salado
△6960m Aconcagua
River Paraná
River Plate
Pampa
ATLANTIC OCEAN
PACIFIC OCEAN
Juan Fernandez Islands
Valdés Peninsula
Patagonia
Falkland Islands
Tierra del Fuego
Cape Horn
South Georgia
SOUTHERN OCEAN
N

Modified Gall Projection
© Oxford University Press

Antarctica has 90% of all of the ice in the world.

Scale

340 km ▷ One centimetre on the map measures 340 kilometres on the ground.

one cm

| 0 | 340 | 680 | 1020 | 1360 km |

Look at the size of the British Isles compared to Antarctica

Area   13 340 000 sq km

Highest point
Vinson Massif   5 140 m

World's longest glacier
Lambert Glacier   400 km

the South Pole

0°

Atlantic Ocean

Prime Meridian

Southern Ocean

60°S

Indian Ocean

Antarctic Circle

South Orkney Islands

Falkland Islands

60°W

ARGENTINA

CHILE

South Shetland Islands

Weddell Sea

Queen Maud Land

60°E

Larsen Ice Shelf

Antarctic Peninsula

Filchner Ice Shelf

Ronne Ice Shelf

80°S

Lambert Glacier

Mount Menzies

Bellingshausen Sea

Vinson Massif

South Pole

Elsworth Land

Wilkes Land

Southern Ocean

Pacific Ocean

Mount Kirkpatrick

Marie-Byrd Land

80°S

Ross Ice Shelf

Mount Markham

120°W

Amundsen Sea

Mount Erebus

120°E

Ross Sea

Key

CHILE   the names of countries are shown in this type of lettering

⎯⎯⎯   country boundary

▲   peak or highest point

△△   mountains

▨   thick ice cap

sea covered by ice all year

sea covered by ice for part of the year

⚑   scientists live here all year

60°S

180°

Southern Ocean

60°S

Zenithal Equidistant Projection
© Oxford University Press

Most of the Arctic is a huge frozen ocean.

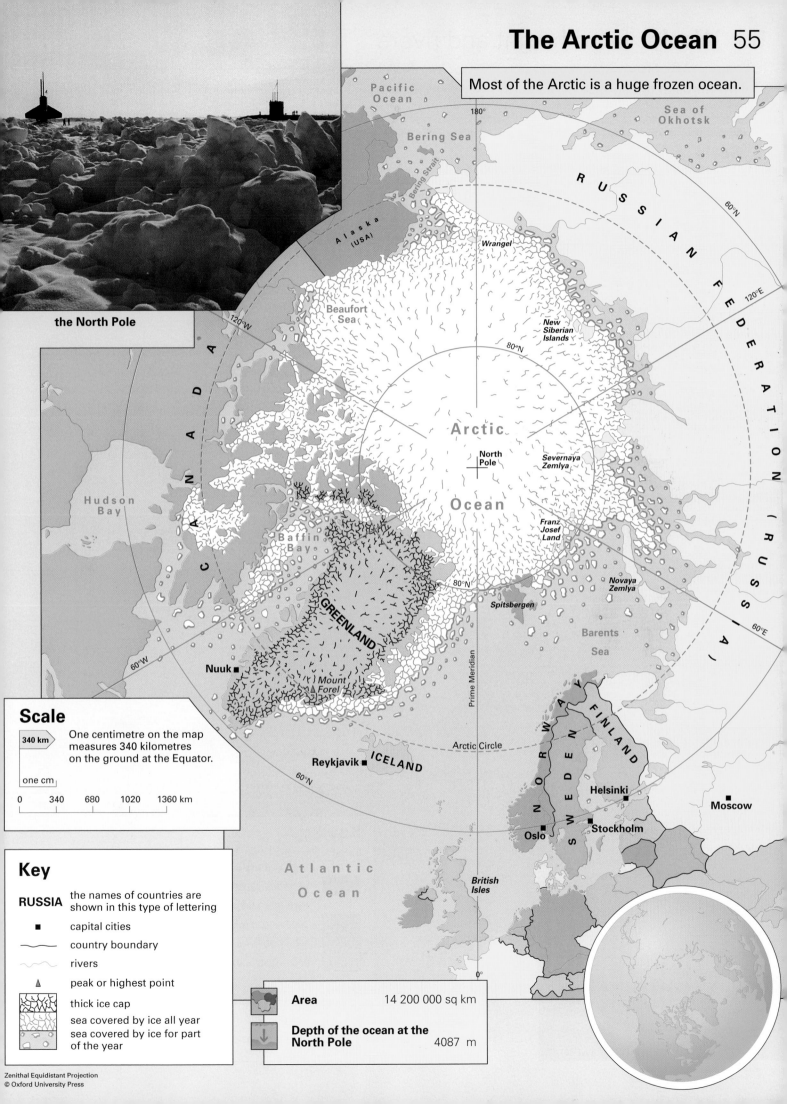

the North Pole

Scale

340 km

One centimetre on the map measures 340 kilometres on the ground at the Equator.

one cm

| 0 | 340 | 680 | 1020 | 1360 km |

Key

RUSSIA   the names of countries are shown in this type of lettering

■   capital cities

⌁   country boundary

⌁   rivers

▲   peak or highest point

   thick ice cap

   sea covered by ice all year

   sea covered by ice for part of the year

Area   14 200 000 sq km

Depth of the ocean at the North Pole   4087 m

Zenithal Equidistant Projection
© Oxford University Press

Map labels

Pacific Ocean

Bering Sea

Sea of Okhotsk

RUSSIAN FEDERATION (RUSSIA)

60°N

120°E

180°

Wrangel

Alaska (USA)

Beaufort Sea

New Siberian Islands

80°N

Severnaya Zemlya

North Pole

Arctic Ocean

Franz Josef Land

CANADA

Hudson Bay

Baffin Bay

GREENLAND

Mount Forel ▲

Nuuk ■

80°N

Novaya Zemlya

Spitsbergen

Barents Sea

60°E

Prime Meridian

120°W

60°W

Reykjavik ■   ICELAND

Arctic Circle

60°N

NORWAY   SWEDEN   FINLAND

Helsinki ■

Oslo ■   Stockholm ■

Moscow ■

Atlantic Ocean

British Isles

0°

Two-thirds of the surface of the earth is covered with water. The rest is land.

Scale

1050 km

One centimetre on the map measures 1050 kilometres on the ground at the Equator.

one cm

| 0 | 1050 | 2100 | 3150 | 4200 km |

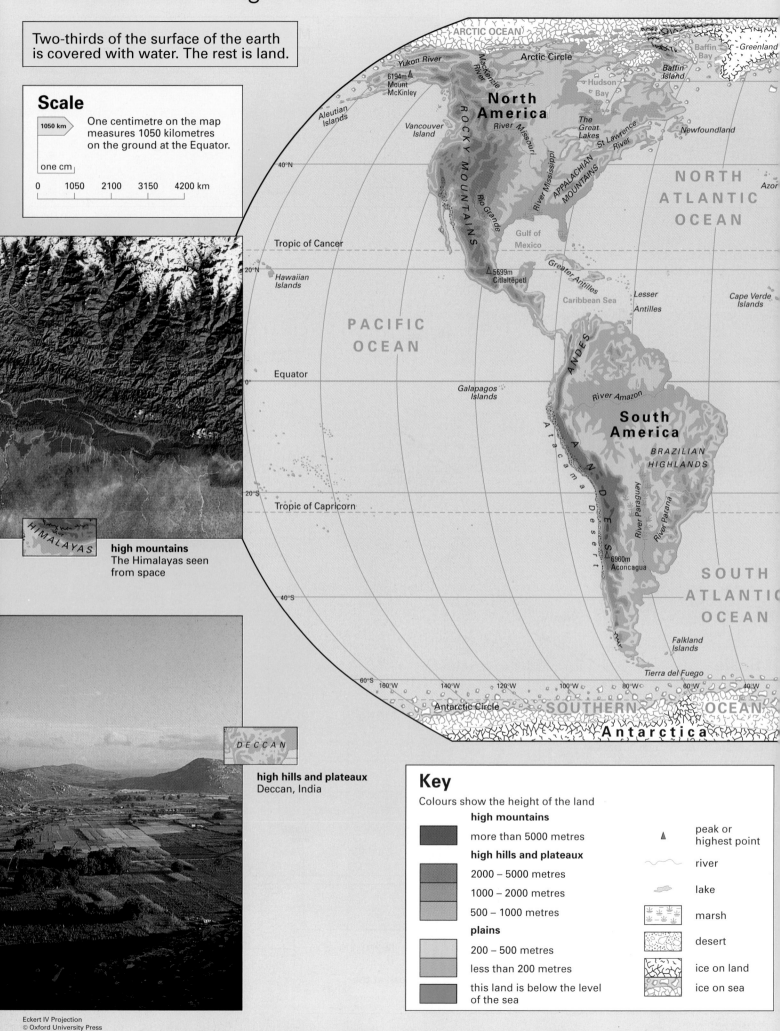

high mountains
The Himalayas seen from space

HIMALAYAS

DECCAN

high hills and plateaux
Deccan, India

Eckert IV Projection
© Oxford University Press

ARCTIC OCEAN

Greenland

Arctic Circle

Baffin Bay

Yukon River

6194m Mount McKinley

Mackenzie River

Baffin Island

Aleutian Islands

Vancouver Island

North America

ROCKY MOUNTAINS

River Missouri

Hudson Bay

The Great Lakes

St Lawrence River

Newfoundland

40°N

River Mississippi

APPALACHIAN MOUNTAINS

NORTH ATLANTIC OCEAN

Rio Grande

Azor

Tropic of Cancer

20°N

Gulf of Mexico

Hawaiian Islands

△5699m Citlaltépetl

Greater Antilles

Lesser Antilles

Cape Verde Islands

PACIFIC OCEAN

Caribbean Sea

Equator

Galapagos Islands

River Amazon

South America

0°

20°S

Tropic of Capricorn

A N D E S

Atacama Desert

BRAZILIAN HIGHLANDS

River Paraguay

River Parana

SOUTH ATLANTIC OCEAN

40°S

△6960m Aconcagua

Falkland Islands

60°S

160°W   140°W   120°W   100°W   80°W   60°W   40°W

Tierra del Fuego

Antarctic Circle

SOUTHERN   OCEAN

Antarctica

Key

Colours show the height of the land

high mountains

more than 5000 metres

high hills and plateaux

2000 – 5000 metres

1000 – 2000 metres

500 – 1000 metres

plains

200 – 500 metres

less than 200 metres

this land is below the level of the sea

▲ peak or highest point

river

lake

marsh

desert

ice on land

ice on sea

ARCTIC OCEAN

Iceland

Barents
Sea

60°N

North
Sea

British
Isles

Europe

R. Rhine

River Danube

4807m
Mont
Blanc

ALPS

Pripet
Marshes

URAL MOUNTAINS

River Volga

Mount
Elbrus
5642m

Black Sea

TAURUS
MOUNTAINS

CAUCASUS

Aral
Sea

Caspian
Sea

Mediterranean Sea

ATLAS MOUNTAINS

ZAGROS MOUNTAINS

Sahara Desert

River Nile

Red Sea

Yenisey River

River Ob

River Irtysh

ALTAI MOUNTAINS

Asia

Gobi Desert

Communism
Peak
7495m

8611m
K2

TIBETAN
PLATEAU

HIMALAYAS

8848m
Mount Everest

DECCAN

River Ganges

Arabian
Sea

Bay of
Bengal

River Lena

Lake
Baykal

Sea of
Okhotsk

Bering Sea

40°N

Hwang-Ho River

River Yangtze

Mekong River

Honshu

East
China
Sea

Tropic of Cancer

PACIFIC
OCEAN

20°N

South
China
Sea

Philippines

Caroline Islands

Marshall
Islands

Equator

Lake
Chad

River Niger

Africa

River Congo

Lake
Victoria

5895m
Mount
Kilimanjaro

Lake
Tanganyika

Lake
Nyasa
(Malawi)

River Zambezi

Seychelles

INDIAN
OCEAN

Madagascar

Sumatra

Java

Borneo

New
Guinea

4508m
Mount
Wilhelm

Solomon
Islands

Oceania

Fiji
Islands

SOUTH
ATLANTIC
OCEAN

Namib Desert

Okavango
Swamp

Kalahari
Desert

Great Sandy
Desert

Great Victoria
Desert

NULLARBOR PLAIN

River Darling

Murray R.

GREAT DIVIDING RANGE

New
Caledonia

Tropic of Capricorn

20°S

North
Island

40°S

Prime Meridian

Tasmania

Tasman
Sea

South
Island

3764m
Mount
Cook

160°E

180°

SOUTHERN OCEAN

20°E   40°E   60°E   80°E   100°E   120°E   140°E

Antarctica

40°W   20°W   0°   20°E   40°E

Prime Meridian

60°W

Weddell
Sea

60°E

80°W

80°E

5140m
Vinson
Massif

▶ **South
Pole**

100°W

100°E

Ross
Sea

120°W

120°E

140°W   160°W   180°   160°E   140°E

Antarctic Circle

River Amazon

plains
The basin of the
River Amazon, Brazil

Patterns of temperature and rainfall throughout the year make types of climate.

Scale

One centimetre on the map measures 1050 kilometres on the ground at the Equator.

one cm

```
0    1050   2100   3150   4200 km
```

Key

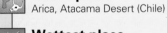

polar climate

continental climate

coastal climate

Mediterranean climate

desert climate

tropical climate

equatorial climate

high mountain climate

* places with record breaking climates

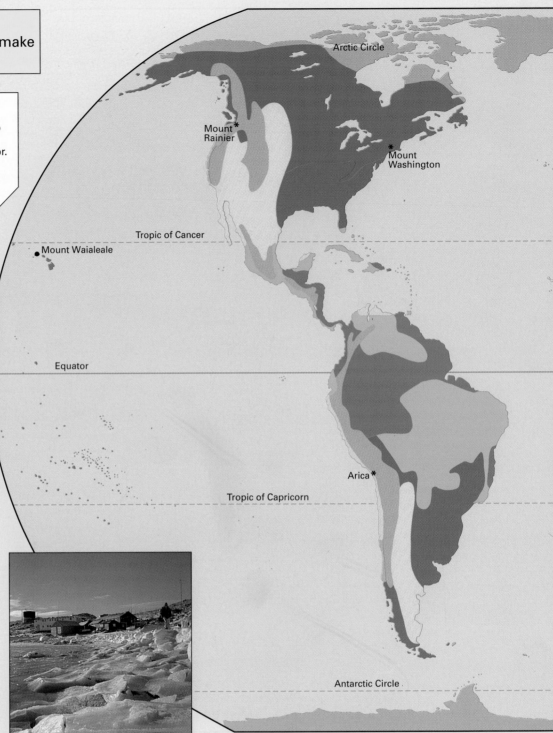

Arctic Circle

Mount Rainier*

Mount Washington*

Tropic of Cancer

Mount Waialeale

Equator

Arica*

Tropic of Capricorn

Antarctic Circle

Eckert IV Projection   © Oxford University Press

Hottest place
Al' Aziziyah (Libya)

Coldest place
Vostok (Antarctica)

Driest place
Arica, Atacama Desert (Chile)

Wettest place
Mount Waialeale (Hawaii)

Windiest place
Mount Washington (USA)

Snowiest place
Mount Ranier (USA)

polar climate
very cold all year

continental climate
very cold winters, warmer summers

coastal climate
warm summers, mild winters, rain all year

Mediterranean climate
hot dry summers, warm wet winters

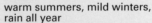

© Oxford University Press

Arctic Circle

Al' Aziziyah *

Tropic of Cancer

Equator

Prime Meridian

Tropic of Capricorn

Antarctic Circle

Vostok
*

tropical climate
very hot all year with a wet season and a dry season

high mountain climate
becomes colder with height

equatorial climate
very hot and wet all year

desert climate
very dry all year

Environments are our natural surroundings.

Scale

One centimetre on the map measures 1050 kilometres on the ground at the Equator.

| 1050 km |
| one cm |

| 0 | 1050 | 2100 | 3150 | 4200 km |

Key

⛰	high mountains
🌲	cold forest
🌳	savannah
🌳	hot forest
▦	desert
▦	marsh
▦	ice on land
▦	ice on the sea
▦	very large built up areas
〜	country boundary

Most environments have been influenced by people.

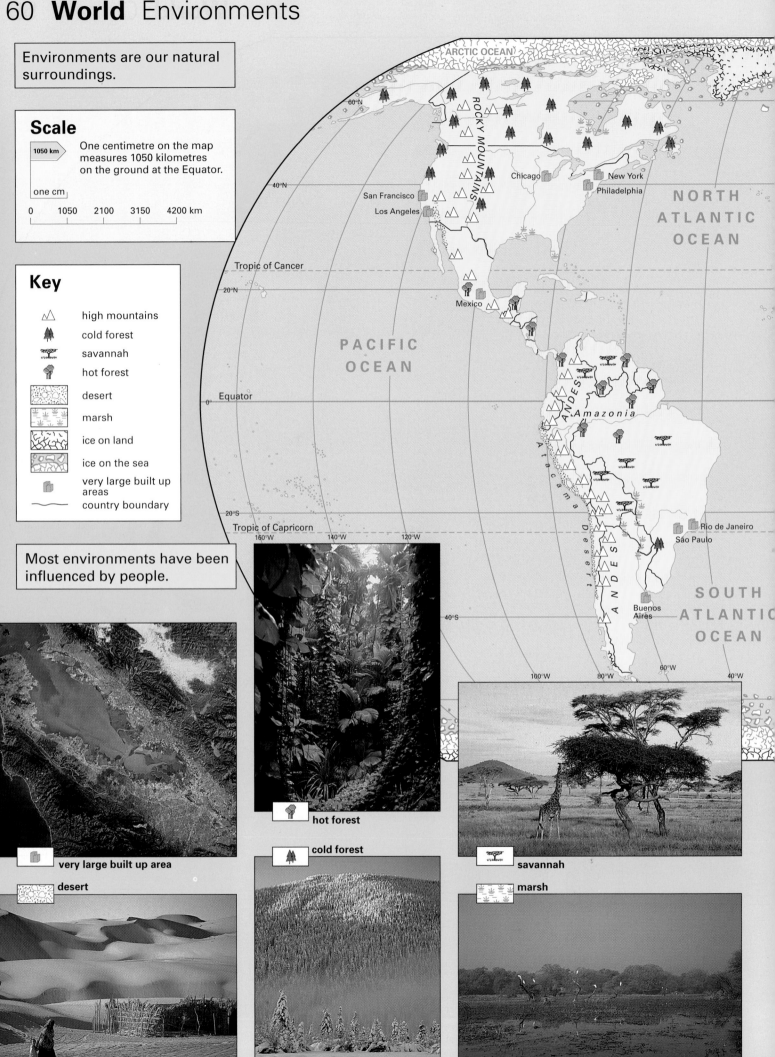

hot forest

cold forest

savannah

very large built up area

desert

marsh

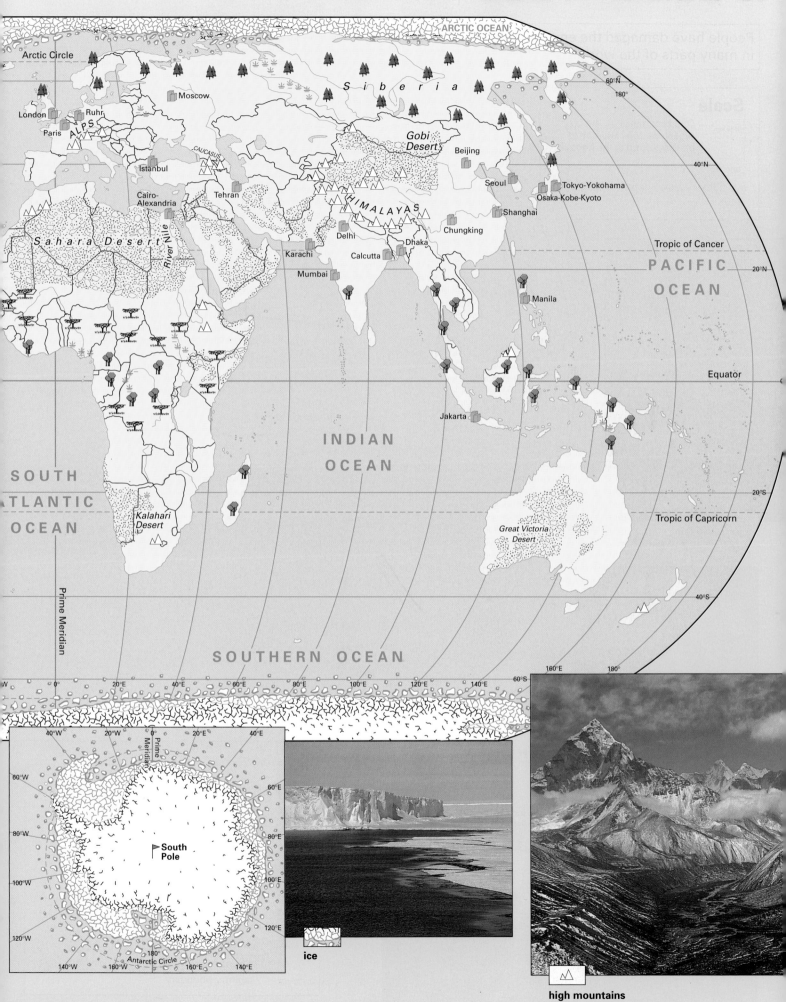

ARCTIC OCEAN

Arctic Circle

S i b e r i a

Moscow

London
Ruhr
ALPS
Paris

*Gobi
Desert*

Beijing

CAUCASUS

Istanbul

Seoul

Tokyo-Yokohama
Osaka-Kobe-Kyoto

Tehran

HIMALAYAS

Shanghai

Cairo-
Alexandria

Chungking

River Nile

Delhi

Dhaka

Sahara Desert

Karachi
Calcutta

Mumbai

Manila

60°N
180°

40°N

Tropic of Cancer

PACIFIC

20°N

OCEAN

**INDIAN
OCEAN**

Jakarta

Equator

SOUTH

ATLANTIC

OCEAN

*Kalahari
Desert*

*Great Victoria
Desert*

20°S

Tropic of Capricorn

Prime Meridian

0°   20°E   40°E   60°E   80°E   100°E   120°E   140°E

160°E   180°

40°S

SOUTHERN OCEAN

60°S

40°W   20°W   0°   20°E   40°E

Prime Meridian

60°W

60°E

80°W

80°E

South
Pole

100°W

100°E

120°W

120°E

140°W   160°W   180°   160°E   140°E

Antarctic Circle

ice

high mountains

Eckert IV Projection
© Oxford University Press

People have damaged the environment in many parts of the world.

Scale

One centimetre on the map measures 1050 kilometres on the ground at the Equator.

1050 km

one cm

| 0 | 1050 | 2100 | 3150 | 4200 km |

acid rain
Jelenia Gora, Poland

nuclear accident
Chernobyl, Ukraine

forest loss
Trans-Amazonian Highway, Brazil

ARCTIC OCEAN

Arctic Circle

Exxon
Valdez
1989

The
Great
Plains

Three
Mile
Island
1979

NORTH
ATLANTIC
OCEAN

Tropic of Cancer

Gulf of
Mexico

Caribbean Sea

PACIFIC
OCEAN

Equator

Atacama Desert

SOUTH
ATLANTIC
OCEAN

Tropic of Capricorn

Antarctic Circle

SOUTHERN   OCEAN

Key

- tropical rain forest
- worst areas of forest loss
- desert
- spreading edges of desert
- areas most affected by acid rain
- sea areas most likely to be affected by major oil pollution
- ✱ recent major oil spill
- ✲ recent major nuclear or chemical accident
- country boundary

Eckert IV Projection
© Oxford University Press

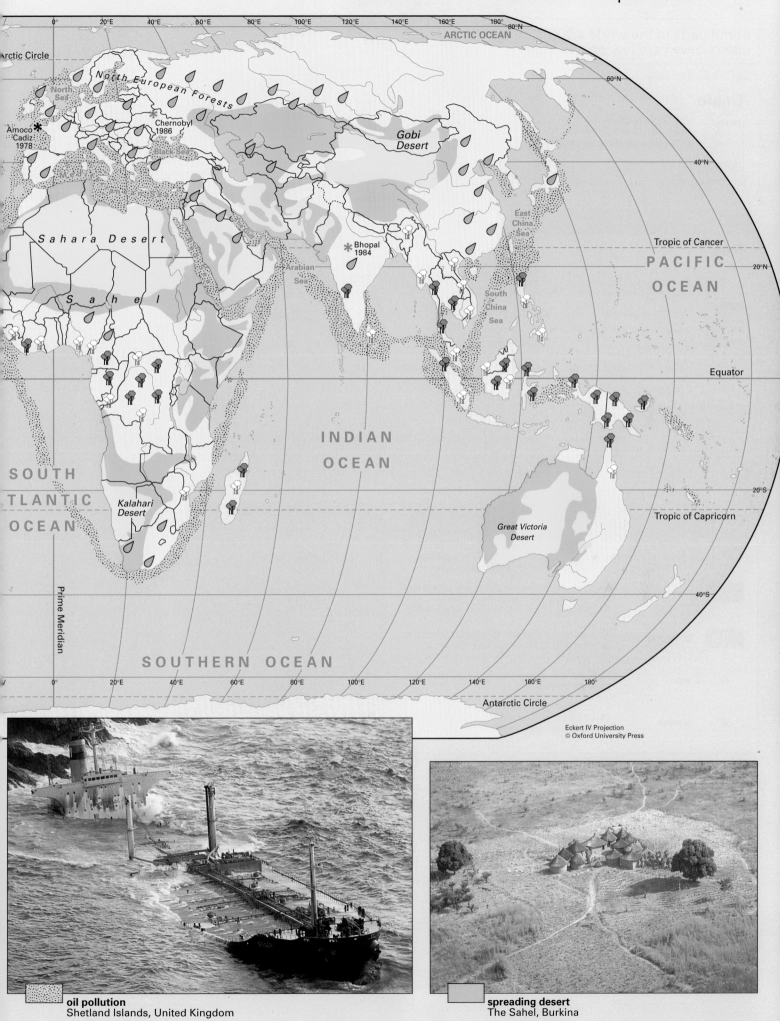

ARCTIC OCEAN

Arctic Circle

North European Forests

North Sea

*
Amoco
Cadiz
1978

Chernobyl
1986

Black Sea

Gobi
Desert

East
China
Sea

Tropic of Cancer

PACIFIC

OCEAN

Sahara Desert

Sahel

*
Bhopal
1984

Arabian
Sea

South
China
Sea

Equator

SOUTH

ATLANTIC

OCEAN

INDIAN

OCEAN

Kalahari
Desert

Great Victoria
Desert

Tropic of Capricorn

Prime Meridian

SOUTHERN OCEAN

Antarctic Circle

Eckert IV Projection
© Oxford University Press

oil pollution
Shetland Islands, United Kingdom

spreading desert
The Sahel, Burkina

Some parts of the world are crowded, others have very few people.

Scale

1050 km

One centimetre on the map measures 1050 kilometres on the ground at the equator.

one cm

| 0 | 1050 | 2100 | 3150 | 4200 km |

Key

one million (1 000 000) people live near each dot

very many people

many people

few people

the world's largest cities. Each has more than 5 million people

Welfare

Some people in the world are rich. Many people are poor, or hungry, or suffering as a result of war.

rich countries — This colour shows the 25 richest countries in the world. Not everyone in these countries is rich but most live comfortably.

poor countries — This colour shows the 40 poorest countries in the world. Not everyone in these countries is poor but most are in need.

war — This symbol shows places where there has recently been a war.

famine — This symbol shows places where there has recently been a shortage of food.

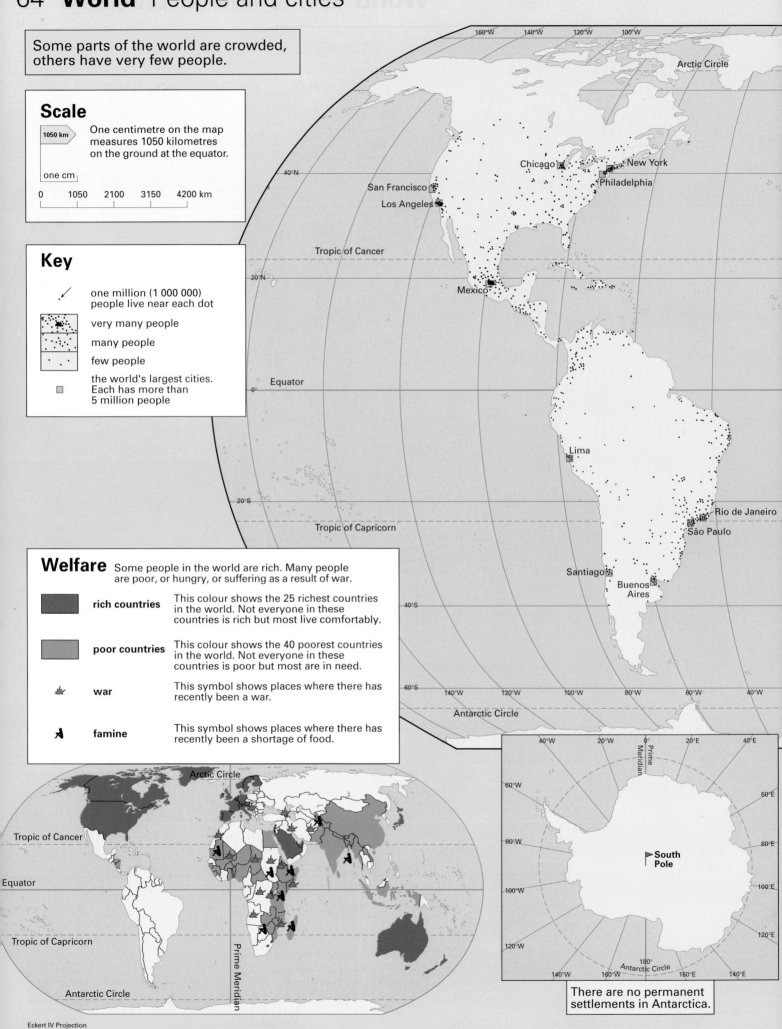

There are no permanent settlements in Antarctica.

Eckert IV Projection
© Oxford University Press

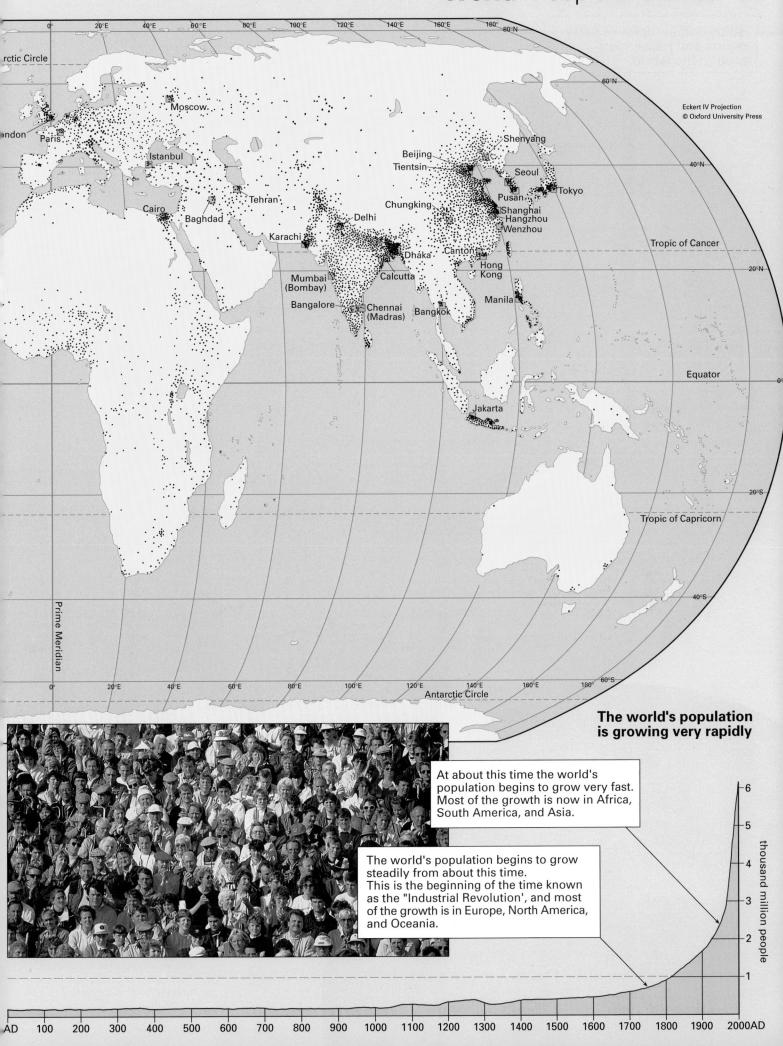

Eckert IV Projection
© Oxford University Press

The world's population is growing very rapidly

At about this time the world's population begins to grow very fast. Most of the growth is now in Africa, South America, and Asia.

The world's population begins to grow steadily from about this time.
This is the beginning of the time known as the "Industrial Revolution', and most of the growth is in Europe, North America, and Oceania.

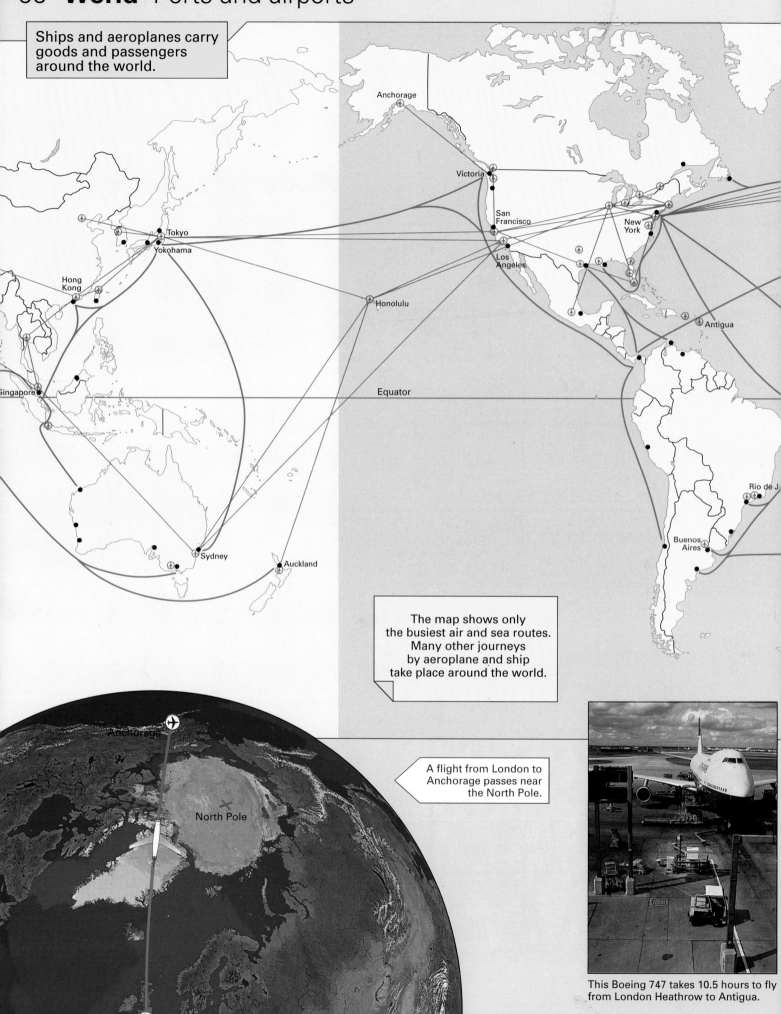

Ships and aeroplanes carry goods and passengers around the world.

Anchorage

Victoria

San Francisco

New York

Tokyo

Yokohama

Hong Kong

Los Angeles

Honolulu

Antigua

Singapore

Equator

Rio de J

Buenos Aires

Sydney

Auckland

The map shows only the busiest air and sea routes. Many other journeys by aeroplane and ship take place around the world.

Anchorage

North Pole

A flight from London to Anchorage passes near the North Pole.

London

This Boeing 747 takes 10.5 hours to fly from London Heathrow to Antigua.

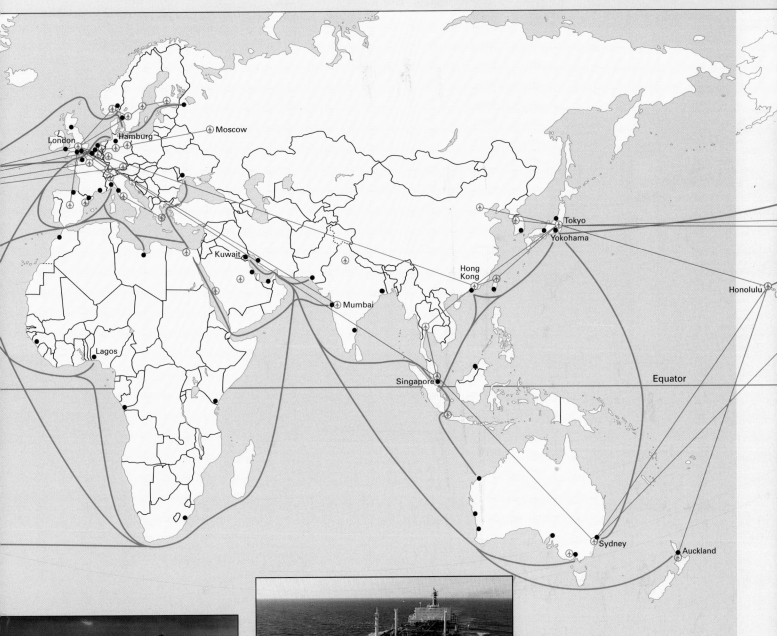

Moscow

Hamburg

London

Kuwait

Mumbai

Lagos

Hong Kong

Tokyo

Yokohama

Honolulu

Singapore

Equator

Sydney

Auckland

This oil tanker takes 18 days to sail from Kuwait to the United Kingdom.

s container ship takes 25 days to sail m Hamburg to Buenos Aires.

Scale

| 1200 km | One centimetre on the map measures 1200 kilometres on the ground at the Equator. |

one cm

| 0 | 1200 | 2400 | 3600 | 4800 km |

Key

———— international boundary

———— main shipping lanes

• major port

main air routes

major airport

It is about 40 000 kilometres (25 000 miles) around the world.

Gall Projection
© Oxford University Press

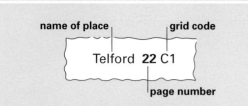

name of place   grid code

Telford **22** C1

page number